From Brian
February 1970

TYNESIDE PORTRAITS

TYNESIDE PORTRAITS

STUDIES IN ART AND LIFE

By

LYALL WILKES

'He was, one might say, provincial in the sense that George Eliot and Cezanne were, and his strength derived from an intimate knowledge of the landscape he chose to paint ... Some minds have achieved greatness in Art not by straining at horizons, but by narrowing their range in order to understood properly a single fragment of locality.'
—Carlos Peacock.
John Constable, *The Man and His Work*.

FRANK GRAHAM
6, Queen's Terrace, Newcastle upon Tyne, 2

© Lyall Wilkes 1971

SBN 902833 93 6

Composed in 11-pt on 12-pt Plantin and printed in Great Britain by Northumberland Press Limited, Gateshead

*To the memory
of
Dr Alan Ruffman
whose devoted skill and kindness
is
remembered by so many*

LIST OF CONTENTS

		page
1	ROBERT TROLLAP (or TROLLOP) (died 1686)	5
2	CHARLES AVISON (1709-1770)	13
3	THOMAS BEWICK AND THE BEILBY FAMILY Thomas Bewick (1753-1828) William Beilby senior (1706-1765) William Beilby junior (1740-1819) Ralph Beilby (1743-1817) Mary Beilby (1749-1797)	39
4	THOMAS MILES RICHARDSON (senior) (1784-1848)	73
5	RICHARD GRAINGER (1797-1861)	103
6	JOHN DOBSON (1787-1865)	123
7	WILLIAM BELL SCOTT (1811-1890)	135
8	JACK COMMON (1903-1968)	153

LIST OF PLATES

Between pages 20-37

The Guildhall, Newcastle.
Capheaton Hall.
Capheaton Hall. Painting.
Capheaton Hall. East Doorway.
Capheaton Hall. South Doorway.
Bockenfield Manor House.
Swarland Old Hall.
Callaly Castle.
Charles Avison.
Thomas Bewick. Portrait.
Thomas Bewick. Banknote design.
Thomas Bewick. Tailpieces.
Thomas Bewick. Tailpieces.
Thomas Bewick. Trade engravings.
Beilby Glass.
Beilby Glass.

Between pages 52-69

Beilby Glass.
Beilby Glass.
Beilby Glass.
Beilby Decorated Bowl.
T. M. Richardson. Portrait.
Newcastle from Gateshead Fell. Painting.

LIST OF PLATES

Evening on the Tyne. Painting.
Grainger Street. Painting.
Lion Bridge, Alnwick. Painting.
Richard Grainger. Portrait.
Bank of England.
Theatre Royal, Grey Street.
Grey Street, Newcastle.
Grey Street, Newcastle.
Grey Street, Newcastle. Print.
Longhirst Hall.

Between pages 84-101

Eldon Square.
John Dobson. Portrait.
Prestwick Lodge.
Nunnykirk. Garden Front.
Nunnykirk. Garden Front.
Nunnykirk. Hall.
Longhirst Hall. Interior.
Meldon Park.
Meldon Park. Garden Front.
Monkwearmouth Station.
William Bell Scott. Portrait.
William Bell Scott. Portrait.
Pauline, Lady Trevelyan.
W. B. Scott, Rossetti, John Ruskin.
Still Life by W. B. Scott.
Jack Common.

TYNESIDE PORTRAITS

INTRODUCTION

ALTHOUGH the lives of the men portrayed in this book reach back from 1968 into the early seventeenth century, and although their achievements were in many forms of Art, a great part of all their very different lives was lived under the shadow of the lantern tower of St Nicholas and of the Old Castle, either in fact, or—as in the case of Jack Common—in imagination. And it seems to me, when I consider them today, this gives their lives a unity; and an underlying theme of this book is really the continuing character and life of Newcastle upon Tyne itself, this city so melodramatically situated on the steep bank of the Tyne within sight of the Cheviot Hills, and the last city in England before the Scottish frontier is reached.

As I walk around the city today and think of the achievements of these men and look at the beauty of their fast disappearing buildings, it is still possible to retain a strong sense of their presence. I can still visualize them walking and talking in the same streets in which I walk, but this sense of continuity with any past is now rapidly being destroyed by the execrable concrete of the modern age.

Dr Thomas Sharp, an architect and planner gifted with the sensibility to raise planning to the rare level of the art it should be, and without which it becomes a communal menace, said:[1]

> 'There is a deplorable ignorance and lack of appreciation in the south of England for what is good in the north.... A book was published the other week on English Houses, and amongst its crowding illustrations it did not contain a single

[1] Anniversary Address to the Ancient Monument Society delivered at York on 7th June, 1969.

example from all the wide territory north of Lincolnshire. Something only a little less prejudiced occurs in almost all the books of this kind ... I find this widely prevalent prejudice, one can even say blindness and bigotry both sad and infuriating ...'

When one thinks of the novels that today receive critical acclaim it would take a Swift to do justice to the neglect of Jack Common—and one knows that had any novelist written with a fraction of his genius about London or some more fashionable city farther south, his work today would not be unrecognized and out of print.

The incomparable Richard Grainger, the first planner of a great (and the best) city centre in England, had been very little written or thought about for over a hundred years after his death; that is why in 1964 I decided (with Gordon Dodds) that a book should be written about him. Even today no architectural historian has begun the detailed study which John Dobson's classical country houses deserve. No critical assessment of T. M. Richardson has been attempted, and Martin Hardie in the most authoritative book on English Watercolours yet published, confuses his work with that of his son, places him in the lowest possible company with artists with whom he has nothing in common, and denies that he is worth serious attention. Well might T. M. Richardson say with regret towards the end of his career, 'One of the grand mistakes of my life has been my neglecting to take up my residence in London twenty or thirty years ago'. Charles Avison wrote many delightful works, one of his melodies being recently described[2] as 'one of the most beautiful as well as one of the saddest of all old English airs'—but it is not to be found in the record catalogues today. Only Thomas Bewick's genius was such that although he refused to move south —'I would even enlist for a soldier or go and herd sheep at five shillings per week as long as I lived, rather than be tied to live in London'—he nevertheless succeeded in winning fame in his lifetime, although he died worth less than £2,000, and his

---

[2] By Charles Cudworth, Curator of The Pendelbury Library of Music, Cambridge, in a Broadcast on 10th May, 1970, referring to part of the 2nd Movement of the Concerto in E Minor.

INTRODUCTION 3

Memoir has never been published in full, nor have his letters been collected and published.[3]

I would like to express my thanks for the assistance I have received from so many people without which this book would not have been possible—especially to J. M. Dent and Son Ltd, for permission to use the long extracts from Jack Common's *Kiddars Luck* and *The Ampersand*; to Cedric Chivers Ltd, for permission to quote from a previous essay of mine on Common, to Irene Palmer for permission to quote from Common's letters to her and for supplying the photograph, and to Sid Chaplin for drawing my attention to the existence of these letters and for his personal recollections of him.

Since domestic architecture features so prominently in these pages I am greatly indebted to the owners or occupiers of houses, who have allowed me to include photographs of the interiors of their homes here—and this means that my particular thanks are due to Sir Charles Orde of Nunnykirk, and to Mr Wintle and Mr Sidney Arkle of Longhirst Hall School, and to Mr and Mrs I. S. Duncan of Prestwick Lodge. To Mr John Browne-Swinburne of Capheaton Hall, and to the University of Newcastle upon Tyne, my thanks are due for permission to include the photograph of Crossby's beautiful painting of Trollap's Capheaton Hall as it was when Trollap completed it, and before the modifications of the eighteenth century had been made.

Many other acknowledgements are to be found in the text of the debt I owe to others for their previous work; but in particular my indebtedness must be acknowledged to David Malley and A. A. Tait for their researches on Trollap, to Dr Arthur Milner for his work on Avison, and to the late Mrs Lona Mosk Packer for her many years of research on Christina Rossetti and William Bell Scott, culminating in her great biography of Christina Rossetti, published in 1963.

As to the photographs, I would particularly like to pay tribute to the assistance I have received from the Oriel Press, Newcastle; and this book owes much to Mr Frank Graham, the Newcastle publisher, who has made available several rare and beautiful plates, and to Mr Gilbert Cockburn not only for the photographs he took himself but for his general advice on photographic prob-

[3] Mr Iain Bain is engaged on work to remedy these omissions.

lems. My particular thanks are also due to Mr Collingwood Stevenson, the Director of the Laing Art Gallery, for permission to use the portrait of T. M. Richardson, and for permitting photographs to be taken of works by T. M. Richardson and William Bell Scott in the Gallery Collection, and to Miss Nerys Johnson who, as always, has been most helpful. As the acknowledgements on the plates will indicate, the Editor of *Country Life* has been particularly generous in supplying photographs, as has the Victoria and Albert Museum, so rich in its collection of Beilby glass. To the National Trust I give my thanks for allowing me to photograph and include the portrait of Pauline Trevelyan by William Bell Scott, which is at Wallington, and to the Scottish National Portrait Gallery for permission to reproduce the portrait of W. B. Scott by his brother David Scott, and the self portrait of W. B. Scott, both from their permanent collection.

To Gordon Dodds, Michael Chaplin and Iain Bain I am indebted for information; and to Mr A. Wallace, Newcastle City Librarian, and Mr Charles Parrish, Librarian of Newcastle Literary and Philosophical Society, I give most grateful thanks for their never failing helpfulness in answering my queries and finding me the books I have required.

LYALL WILKES
Newcastle upon Tyne

CHAPTER ONE

Robert Trollap (or Trollop)[1]

No portrait or likeness of any kind is known of Robert Trollap—and indeed not very much is known about him at all. But it is not true, as has sometimes been stated, that he came from a long line of stone-masons in York. The researches of David Malley[2] have revealed that in the York House Books (the Minutes of the Common Council) of May 1648, it was 'ordered that Robert Trollap a free mason be admitted a freeman of this citty paying £8 he haveinge ingaged himselfe not to work on his bricklayers trade'. This entry tells us that Robert's father was not a freeman of York, otherwise Robert would not have had to become a freeman by purchase, but would have become one through his father, as Robert's son Henry did in York without payment in 1669.[3] In those days in York a man could not practise the trade of mason within the city without being a freeman. Robert became a freeman of Newcastle on 25th September, 1657, in the year when he finished building the new Newcastle Exchange (or Guildhall as it was later called), his son Henry became a freeman of Newcastle in 1671, as did his youngest son Robert in 1690.[4]

We do not yet know the date of Robert Trollap's birth, why he left his bricklaying trade for that of mason, why he came to Newcastle from York, or from what year he took over the design-

---

[1] Robert Trollap is the way he wrote his own name and therefore is the spelling which is here preferred: his name on some accounts (e.g. Capheaton) appears as Trollup.

[2] A student of the Department of Architecture, University of Newcastle upon Tyne.

[3] See The Surtees Society, Freemen of York, Vo. 2, Volume 102, p. 136, published in 1899.

[4] See the Register of Freemen of Newcastle upon Tyne in the Newcastle City Archives.

ing of buildings as distinct from working under the direction and to the design of others. All the buildings that are at present attributed to him by virtue of their characteristic style and individual stone relief work were built between 1656 and 1676—which leaves long gaps in his early middle years and towards the end of his life in 1686 without any attributable building.

In respect of only two buildings is there at present any documentary evidence that he was the designer and builder. These are the Newcastle Exchange (now known as the Guildhall) contracted to be built by Trollap for £2,000 and built between 1656 and 1657, and Capheaton Hall which he built for Sir John Swinburne between 1668 and 1670 for the price of £500, this house symbolizing the re-emergence of the Swinburnes, who had been on the Royalist side in the Civil War, from Puritan disfavour into the baronetcy conferred in 1661.

It may be that Trollap was unfortunate in that during his middle years the prevailing attitude in the Commonwealth was not one which viewed decorative building with much favour—and this may partially explain why there is no trace of a Trollap building before 1656. But whilst there is only documentary evidence of Trollap's authorship of the two already mentioned buildings, the stylistic evidence that he was also the designer and architect of Swarland Old Hall, Bockenfield Manor House and Callaly Castle is overwhelming: and with all respect to the views expressed by Professor Pevsner[5] and A. A. Tait,[6] I have no doubt but that Netherwitton Hall is another Trollap house. There cannot have been working in Northumberland between 1656 and 1686 two such extroverted eccentric rural classicists each decorating their walls with elaborate stone carvings of fruit, leaf, and vine, or vases of flowers, each delighting in richly decorated sundials on the sides of their houses and—most characteristic of all —each employing an intertwining cable design or spiral fluting around door surrounds, around windows, around coats of arms —around anything. When human figures and faces are carved they are somewhat grotesque in a kindly rural sort of way, and all the buildings attributable to him reflect the same forthright

[5] *The Buildings of Northumberland*, p. 217 (Penguin Books).
[6] Classicism in Eccentric Form by A. A. Tait (*Country Life*, 12th August, 1965).

uninhibited love of elaborate work in stone, combined with an unacademic and very early classicism that is a delight. And although there is much less of this exuberant stone work at Netherwitton than in the other houses, there is enough around the sundial and elsewhere to mark its creator as Trollap. It was perhaps the last house he designed, and built at a time when the classical buildings of Wren and others were beginning to be better known. This must have acted as a check upon Trollap's own exuberant version of the classical, and made him become increasingly 'correct'.

Trollap's earliest known building work is generally stated to be his Newcastle Exchange and Guildhall of 1656-1657. Mr Aynesley, the present tenant of Swarland Old Hall, told me that when he came to the house some thirty years ago he could (although with great difficulty) read the date 1638 near the top of the window at the side of the house—and numerals can still be seen there which today are impossible to decipher. If Mr Aynesley's original reading was correct it would pre-date Swarland Old Hall by eighteen years from any other known Trollap work—but the more likely explanation is that the date on Swarland was in fact 1658, very shortly after the Newcastle Guildhall was completed.

Swarland Old Hall does look the earliest of these Trollap houses, the stone work design being more timid and carrying less conviction, but the cable work around the windows and two angel faces above the front door show the designer's hand. Semi-circular pediments are placed over the windows at somewhat too great a distance above them. It was a Manor House of the powerful Heron family from Ford, and the Heron coat of arms showing the three Herons is on the same side of the house as the mysterious date numerals. It must have been a very small Manor House of great beauty, as you can see even today, imagining it without the unfortunate accretions at either side and without the present dormer windows; but it has not the strength or boldness of decoration of Bockenfield.

Mr Aynesley asked if I would like to see the grave of 'the man who had the house built' and we walked over a field to the rear of the house and there in the field was the burial place of the man who must have instructed Trollap to build—the grave of

William Hesilrigge, one of the Northumbrian Covenanters who, the inscription—fast disappearing in 1800 and transferred to a new stone in that year—tells us, died on April 12th, 1681, aged eighty-eight years; so that if the date on the house was 1658 he had enjoyed this exquisite miniature manor house for twenty-three years. As we stood there Mr Aynesley said that 'the talk was' he had come from Ford; and indeed if the Hesilrigges were entitled to put the Heron coat of arms on the house they must have come from Ford where the main Heron stronghold was, and the inscription makes it clear that William Hesilrigge was of no ordinary stock—

> This was the grandson to Esquire
> Yet to lie here was his desire ...

(It is worth remembering that the beautiful Kate Babington whose dissenting activities led to her being refused burial in consecrated ground and so was buried in the garden of Harnham Hall, Northumberland, where her grave may still be seen, was born a Miss Hesilrigge.)

Whether this earliest of all Trollap's known houses was built before the Guildhall of 1658 or, as I think most probable, just after, the Guildhall itself clearly remains, from the engravings we have of it, early Trollap at his most surprising. A. A. Tait in a learned and invaluable article on Trollap[7] quotes the contract with the Corporation as requiring the use of classical elements—'Dorick Capitalls, pilasters and rustication'. Although apparently intended as an attempt at a rare and pre-Wren exercise in classicism, it turned out as Professor Pevsner says[8] 'in a bastard style, with round arches and pointed arches, rustication and crazy gothicizing tracery'. There was even a Gothic rose-window and the whole confection is strongly reminiscent of the somewhat earlier architecture of the Low Countries. The exterior of this building was transformed by the addition of a truly classical front by David Stephenson and William Newton in 1796 but a great

---

[7] *Country Life*, 12th August, 1965.
[8] *The Buildings of England* (Northumberland) by Nikolaus Pevsner and Ian Richmond, p. 49 (Penguin Books).

deal of the Trollap seventeenth-century interior remains and very beautiful it is with the hammer beam ceiling and wall panelling.

After the designing of the Exchange and Swarland Old Hall, Trollap in 1663 completed the building of Christchurch, Tynemouth 'to raise and ceil the roof and to plaster the walls'.[9] Nothing of this work can be seen; but then came the designing of Capheaton Hall, Bockenfield and Callaly Castle where his designs were entirely successful producing three houses of great beauty and rarity—with Capheaton as his masterpiece.

Pevsner[10] assesses Capheaton Hall as 'one of the most interesting houses of its date and character in England and far too little known'. There is the same endearing Trollapian mixture of the by then well known Italianate and classical elements of pediment and pilaster, but they exist side by side with what Trollap himself liked—mullioned windows and dog tooth ornament around the sundials. Yet whilst there is this element of looking back, Trollap's great banded pilasters at Bockenfield and Capheaton reaching roof high are—as A. A. Tait reminds us—reminiscent in their strength and theatricality of Vanbrugh's work fifty years later. How beautiful Capheaton must have looked before the alterations of the eighteenth century is shown by Robert Crossby's painting of 1674. When William Newton (architect of Newcastle's gracious Assembly Rooms of 1776 and the classical church of St Ann's, Newcastle), built the correct if somewhat dull classical façade at the then rear of the house, obliterating Trollap's great pilasters and stone carving to accord with the then less exuberant taste of the gentry, it must have been at that time that the walls and gateway shown on Crossby's painting were demolished and the HA-HA substituted, so that the rear of the house became the front, and the original front path to the front door at which the Lorraines are being welcomed in Crossby's painting fell into disuse and became as it is today.

These alterations remind us that Crossby's painting and Trollap's building belong to an age when Nature was looked upon as something to be kept at bay by walls, or at least by an enclosed

[9] H. M. Colvin, *A Biographical Dictionary of English Architects 1660-1840* (John Murray, 1954), p. 622.
[10] *The Buildings of England* (Northumberland), pp. 111-112 (Penguin Books).

formal garden of intricate design, as different from natural landscape as the art of the gardener could contrive. This was before the gardeners of the eighteenth century, led by Kirkharle's Lancelot ('Capability') Brown, took down the enclosures, landscaped the whole of the surrounding countryside as a natural garden, and allowed it to flow into and take over the formal garden.

That there was a great loss in all this as well as gain can be seen from Crossby's beautiful picture. This painting reminds us once again that the country house with its collections of books, furniture, porcelain and pictures from the time Palladio began building his villas until the last flowering of Georgian elegance and light in Dobson's houses, is the nearest thing to a glimpse of paradise that has yet been created by Man—something to set against all the crimes and horrors he has perpetrated.

A. A. Tait in his article already referred to, tells us that examination of the Capheaton building accounts between 1668-1670 show regular monthly payments of £50 to 'Mr Trollupp', and reveal that the beautiful carving around the windows was the work of one Allen Johnston who must therefore join the other numerous stone carvers and plasterers and joiners working under famous architects of the seventeenth and eighteenth centuries as the real yet unremembered source of much of the architectural pleasure we derive today. Thinking of themselves as prosaic artisans they would have been incredulous had they been told they were artists whose work would evoke admiration and interest nearly three hundred years later.

Callaly Castle began its life as a pele tower, and although remodelled and extended both before and after Trollap's putting in of the new front to the house in 1676, this main front of Trollap's still remains. I have already said there is no (as yet) documentary proof of Trollap's authorship, but examination of the design of the sundial and the design of the stonework on and above the windows, and the size and vigour of the doorway with the coat of arms above it, seems to point indisputably to Trollap —even if to a Trollap more restrained with the passing of the years as compared with his boisterous Bockenfield and Capheaton days.

A. A. Tait somewhat dubiously and with many reservations attributes Netherwitton Hall to Trollap but calls the exterior 'lifeless and dull' and regrets that Trollap's love of ornament was apparently deliberately abandoned at Netherwitton which he finds drab in consequence. I can only say I find the house one of great beauty, and that there is enough of Trollap's imprint on the window heads, in the carving around the sundial, and in the wood carving of the interior to satisfy me that Trollap probably was the designer. It seems to me that Trollap steadily became more conventional in style with the passing of the years and was never again as flamboyant as he had been at Bockenfield, which must have been built before Professor Pevsner's dating of 1675 because, as David Malley has discovered, the Herons sold this house to the Widdringtons in 1672 and the Heron's coat of arms is clearly to be seen on the house. Again, Professor Pevsner put the date of Netherwitton at about 1700-1710—which is at least fourteen years after Trollap's death in 1686—and will only permit himself to say that it is 'in the tradition of Capheaton'.

Without any documentary evidence either way, attribution must be a matter of the visual impression the house makes, but my strong feeling that it is Trollap's design—although it may even have been completed after his death by his youngest son Robert or by someone else—is strengthened by the fact that a present member of the family owning Netherwitton has a strong recollection of seeing a Trollap account in connection with its building amongst the great accumulation of family papers. This is only one of the many matters concerning Trollap's life and work on which it is to be hoped further research will be undertaken.

Trollap lies buried in St Mary's Churchyard in Gateshead—directly opposite to where across the river Tyne stands David Stephenson's classical round church of All Saints. He was predeceased by his son Henry who was buried in St Mary's on 23rd November, 1677. St Mary's Churchyard is a refreshing oasis of green, all the more welcome to the eye since in recent years the area has been increasingly overshadowed by new buildings, new roads, the new bridge and new concrete everywhere. Although Colvin in 1954 stated 'at the East end of the churchyard there is an elaborate monument erected in his lifetime and repaired in 1855-60'—at first sight there does not appear to be any sign of the Trollap monument today. In fact what now appears as the Greene family mausoleum is the tomb of the Trollaps—the Greene family having intermarried with the descendants of Trollap, and being sufficiently convinced of their own importance to see that all reference to the Trollaps disappeared in the alterations of 1855-1860 carried out by a member of the Greene family—or even in an earlier alteration made by them.

Early histories of Newcastle refer to a statue of Trollap formerly standing on top of his monument with his arm pointing towards his Exchange on the opposite side of the river, and say that the following appalling verse was one time inscribed on the monument (perhaps this was an added incentive to the Greene family to obliterate all reference to Trollap)—

> 'Here lies Robert Trollup
> Who made yon stones roll up;
> When death took his soul up
> His body filled this hole up'

That this doggerel was actually written at one time on Trollap's monument (although there is no convincing proof of it) is given some support by the fact that verse as bad as this could not have survived to be quoted in the early histories of Newcastle unless it had been actually inscribed somewhere, and that the admiring words call to mind just such a man as Trollap must have been—a vigorous, self-confident, original kind of man with no portentous solemnity or pretension. His designs for houses with their ornate decorative stonework are without parallel in English architecture, and appreciation of their importance and beauty is only now beginning.

CHAPTER TWO

Charles Avison

'For this Elegance of Taste in the Performance of the Solo, consists not in those agile Motions, or Shiftings of the Hand which strike with Surprise the common Ear, but in the tender and delicate Touches, which to such indeed are least perceptible, but to a pure Ear productive of the highest Delight ... avoid all extravagant Decorations.'

Charles Avison: An Essay on Musical Expression, 1752.

WHEN on a morning visit in 1747 to the shop of Kirkman, the harpsichord maker, the great Fulke Greville enquired whether Kirkman knew of any young musician who was fit company for a gentleman, since he would only wish to receive instruction from 'some one who had mind and cultivation as well as finger and ear; lamenting, with strong contempt, that in the musical tribe, the two latter were generally dislocated from the two former',[1] Greville was only emphasizing—even if the words sound strange on the lips of a descendant of Sir Philip Sidney—the then generally accepted view of a musician as a kind of not very superior servant.

With some trepidation Kirkman recommended, and after interview and cross examination Greville accepted into his household, the youthful Charles Burney who by his social gifts quickly won an honoured place in Greville's household and became his friend and constant companion. It was this Charles Burney who set the seal on his achievements as a composer by publishing in 1776

---

[1] *Memoirs of Dr Burney*, 1832, Vol. 1, p. 26, by his daughter Madame d'Arblay.

the first of the four volumes of his 'General History of Music' which won him renown and the esteem of the leading writers of his day, so that any stigma in being initially a musician and composer, was forgotten in recognition as a successful man of letters and as one of the leading members of Mrs Thrale's circle. For a great part of the second half of the eighteenth century Dr Burney's word was as authoritative in matters of music as was Dr Johnson's in matters of literature.

Yet there had been an earlier composer and critic—Charles Avison—who, partly because he was too dedicated a musician to value the social success which plainly Dr Burney craved and won, and partly because he refused to leave his beloved Newcastle when offered better opportunities nearer London, never quite won Burney's fame, although he became one of the leading figures in the musical world of his day. It was this Charles Avison who not only wrote the first book of purely musical criticism in the English language, which quickly ran into three editions and was translated into German, but who won such a reputation as composer, critic, teacher, and conductor, that, as Dr Arthur Milner has pointed out, he was able to insist that he did not attend upon his pupils at their homes for lessons, but made his pupils attend upon him at his own house, first in Rosemary Lane, and later at Green Court, Newgate Street, near St Andrew's Church.

In his History,[2] Dr Burney refers to Avison as—

'... an ingenius man and an elegant writer upon his art. He visited Italy early in his youth, and at his return having received instruction from Geminiani, a bias in his compositions for violin and in his Essay on Musical Expression, towards that master is manifest. Rameau was likewise his model in harpsichord music, and he over-rated Marcello's Psalms either to depreciate Handel, or to forward the subscription he opened for their publication.[3] He succeeded however in neither of these designs: Handel is more and more respected, and Marcello is dropped into his right place, among eminent dilettanti.'

[2] *General History of Music*, Vol. IV, 1789, p. 670.
[3] In 1757 Avison co-operated with his friend John Garth of Durham in the publication of an edition of Marcello's vocal music.

This reference to Avison is correct in drawing attention to his preference for the Italian school over the German—a preference which so angered the lovers of Handel that an anonymous reply to Avison's Essay on Musical Expression was published in London in 1753 by William Hayes, then Professor of Music at Oxford. It is quite wrong however to suggest that Avison had not a high regard for Handel—his writings contain many tributes to him; but he never fell into idolatry, and his remark that Handel's music was surprisingly good since it was written by 'one who had supplied the town with musical entertainments of every kind for thirty years altogether', did not endear him to Handelians.

What Avison as a musical conservative did not like was the first stirring of expressionistic emotion and passion at the expense of melody, harmony and form—the first stirring of nineteenth-century romanticism. His musical masters in instrumental music were Corelli and his pupil Geminiani, he was as devoted to Scarlatti as he was derisive of Vivaldi, in vocal music he exalted Marcello above all and, in Opera, Rameau. Whatever may be said about these choices, they denote for a Newcastle music master and organist in the mid-eighteenth century, a highly individual choice owing little to fashionable taste. Appended to the many publications of his own music during his lifetime, he attached combative prefaces with a good turn of phrase which made the more urbane Dr Burney shake his head—

'The late Mr Avison attributed the corruption and decay of Music to the torrent of modern symphonies with which we were overwhelmed from foreign countries. But though I can readily subscribe to many of the opinions of that ingenious writer, we differ so widely on this subject, that it has long seemed to me as if the variety, taste, spirit and new effects produced by contrast and the use of crescendo and diminuendo in these symphonies, had been of more service to instrumental Music in a few years, than all the dull and senile imitations of Corelli, Geminiani, and Handel, had been in half a century'.

Charles Avison was born in Newcastle in 1709, baptized at St John's Church on February 16 of that year, his father Richard Avison being 'one of ye Waits' and his mother Ann Avison probably a church organist.[4] After his return from Italy as a young man it is almost certain that he became a pupil of Geminiani who lived for many years in England from 1714 onwards. Avison learned to master and teach the organ, harpsichord, flute and violin although it seems clear from the negligible amount of organ music he wrote that whilst he earned his living as an organist it was an instrument for which he felt no great devotion.

The most important year in Avison's life was 1736, for in that year when he was only twenty-seven years old, he was, on the 12th July, appointed organist at St John's Church, Newcastle, and then only three months later was offered the post of organist at St Nicholas's which he held until his death in 1770. In that same year he also organized the first of the subscription concerts that he was to hold in the Assembly Rooms in the Groat Market, and at other places in the town, until his death—William Newton's present Assembly Rooms not being completed until 1776.

These subscription concerts which Avison organized himself for thirty-four years were the greatest single musical influence in Newcastle throughout that period. If the music played was primarily Italian and French, the balance was frequently redressed by Purcell and Handel and other English and German composers. Avison's friend Felice Giardini, the violinist, made an appearance at these concerts as did the great Geminiani himself, and so later did Avison's former pupil, William Shield of Wylam (1748-1829), second violinist to Giardini at the Italian Opera House, author of twenty operas written for the Haymarket and Covent Garden Theatres, and in 1817 appointed Master of the Musicians-in-Ordinary to the King. Although in 1738 Avison was charging only 2/6d for a ticket which admitted one gentleman or two ladies to a whole series,[5] the researches of Dr Milner have shown that in later years when the concerts were an established success the same ticket cost one guinea which ensured (whether by design or not) that the audience would be composed of gentry and the more prosperous merchants and professional people in the town. His fees for tuition on flute or violin were

---

[4] That these and other facts about Avison are now known is due primarily to the researches of Dr Arthur Milner the Newcastle composer and music critic.

[5] See Welford's *Men of Mark 'Twixt Tyne and Tweed'*, Vol. 1, p. 157.

half a guinea a month with one guinea serving as entrance fee.

Since Avison was paid only £50 a year as organist of St Nicholas's, he had to teach; and those he taught would in time be drafted into his orchestra with a strengthening from professional or semi professional musicians working in the town; and these, with the town members and the gentry coming in from the countryside of Northumberland and Durham for practice, would be rehearsed by Avison in the instrumental and choral items forming the programme of forthcoming subscription concerts. The existence of this orchestra, and the concerts with virtuoso musicians coming from London and elsewhere, must have been a great incentive to Avison to compose music to be performed at them. Charles Cudworth in an article on Avison[6] gives some idea of the extent of his published work by listing some of them—the set of trio sonatas, six sets of concertos for strings, a collection of twenty-six concertos, three sets of harpsichord sonatas with accompaniments for string trio, and twelve concertos arranged from Scarlatti's harpsichord sonatas, and points out that all these were so popular that they went into several editions—with the trenchant prefaces that were the prelude to the publication in 1752 of the Essay on Musical Expression that brought him an even wider fame.

The Essay is well worth reading even at this date, with much shrewd comment on the technicalities of orchestral playing and conducting, and guidance on the best use of harpsichord, bassoon and violin especially. Its reprinting with Avison's other prefaces to his published music is overdue. He has a considerable gift for the almost impossible task of discussing musical problems in literary terms; and he has an engaging honesty and knows that in the end, 'the Energy and Grace of Musical Expression is of too delicate a Nature to be fixed by Words: it is a Matter of Taste rather than of Reasoning, and is, therefore, much better understood by Example than by Precept.'

Avison in temper with the optimism of his time, had no doubt about the beneficial affect of music on the human mind and behaviour, 'I would appeal to any Man, whether ever he found himself urged to acts of Selfishness, Cruelty, Treachery, Revenge

[6] *Musical Times*, May 1970.

or Malevolence by the Power of musical Sounds?' Avison may be right in this, but leaving aside primitive music accompanying savage sacrifice and the martial music of later armies, our world has had occasion recently to ponder the greater problem of why a love of music does not tend to a deeper perception in behaviour, and how it could happen that orchestras were playing great symphonies to audiences within fifty miles of Belsen and Dachau, and how Beethoven today can be played to apparently unaware segregated audiences in South Africa. Whilst the lifeblood of great musicians may not tend to evil action, can it be said that it tends to any good? If music does not tend to make us more imaginative and compassionate, is its sole justification that it gives sensual pleasure?

No doubt a composer may have the most subtle ideas giving rise to the emotion which, to his own satisfaction, he may then express in music of sublime beauty; but the means of communicating all but simple ideas through music are so inadequate and demand such subtle antennae on the part of the listener, that only an infinitesimal part of the idea can be conveyed; and the idea, however beautiful and valid and convincing it may sound as music, can evoke so many contradictory and equally valid interpretations to attentive and intelligent listeners that it may be said—however beautiful the music—that for all practical purposes the idea has been lost. Music is a defective instrument to communicate ideas, but is a most subtle and effective way *to communicate and heighten emotion*. That is why when Beethoven wished to say something more explicit about Freedom he had to write Fidelio.

It is of course ridiculous to complain that Music is not Literature or that it lacks Literature's power to evoke ideas and compassion; but it may be salutory to stress that precisely because of this, great Music like Science and great Painting, and unlike great Literature, *is neutral*, and that it can give as much pleasure to evil men as to good. I do not think that can be said of the novels of Tolstoy or Dickens or of great literature in general. Even in Avison's day the question of the relationship (if any) between a love of beauty, and moral awareness, lay before his eyes in the spectacle of a society which could produce exquisite architecture, furniture, porcelain and music, and hang ten-year-old children for theft. But Avison was fortunate in that problems like these were not in his mind—or in anyone's mind—when he wrote his Essay in 1752.

What, Avison asks, is true Musical Expression in the problem confronting a composer who has to put into musical terms verse by Milton or a Hymn or Song? He answers—'it is such a concurrence of Air and Harmony, as affects us most strongly with the Passions or Affections which the Poet intends to raise: ... the Composer is not principally to dwell on particular Words in the Way of Imitation, but to comprehend the Poet's general Drift or Intention, and on this to form his Airs and Harmony, either by Imitation (so far as Imitation may be proper to this End) or by any other Means. But this I must still add, that if he attempts to raise the Passions by Imitation, it must be such a temperate and chastised Imitation, as rather brings the Object before the Hearer, than such a one as induces him to form a comparison between the Object and the Sound. For in this last case, his Attention will be turned entirely on the Composer's Art, which must effectually check the Passion. The Power of Music is in this respect parallel to the Power of Eloquence: if it works at all, it must work in a secret and unsuspected Manner. In either case a pompous display of Art will destroy its own Intentions ... One of the best general Rules, perhaps, that can be given for Musical Expression, is that which gives rise to the Pathetic in every other art, an unaffected strain of Nature and Simplicity.'

As an organist, Avison writes severely of some other organists condemning those who over-decorated their music, 'But sorry I am to observe that the chief performer in this kind of noble chorus is too often so fond of his own conceits; that with his absurd Graces and tedious and ill connected Interludes, he misleads or confounds his Congregation, instead of being the natural Guide and Director of the whole.'

This Essay brought Avison not only fame in his day but offers of musical posts elsewhere including appointment as organist at York Minster. An ambitious man, in Burney's sense, would have accepted; but quite plainly Avison was so devoted to his concerts and his choral and orchestral teaching in Newcastle that he refused them all and remained in Newcastle until he died. Mondays and Fridays he usually reserved for teaching, Thursdays and Saturdays for the rehearsal and conducting of the orchestra, and in addition to this there would be the direction and rehearsal of the choir at St Nicholas' and the playing of the organ at services on the Sunday.

Richard Welford quotes from a description of a concert of vocal and instrumental music of 29th November, 1739, when 'There were twenty-six instrumental performers, and the proper number of voices from Durham. The gentlemen and ladies joined in the chorus and all present saluted the performers with loud peals of claps, acknowledging a general satisfaction. This was the greatest audience that ever was known on a like occasion in Newcastle.' In 1758 Avison published the scores of twenty-six of his own concertos which proved so popular they were quickly sold out. In the Preface to the Concertos he severely criticized those who 'are only struck with the marvellous. A sudden chromatic chord at once commands their attention while the more natural melody is entirely lost upon them,' and in his last Preface of 1766 he complains of the growing fashion for 'turgid and bombastic' writing in music as well as in literature. It seems clear that he feared his own music, founded on simple melody, would be drowned in the growing clamour, as indeed it was, Dr Burney in 1789 giving his judgement on Avison's music in the fourth volume of his History, in terms which posterity has endorsed on his own music, 'With respect to Avison's own musical productions they want force, correctness, and originality, sufficient to be ranked very high among the works of masters of the first class.'

In spite of Burney's verdict Avison's concertos were regularly played, especially in the North of England, until the middle of the nineteenth century, and Charles Cudworth has recently[7] quoted with approval Vincent Novello's comment on Concerto No. 4, Opus 4, that it was, 'an excellent composition, and the last movement especially is a very tasteful and charming air, appropriately harmonized, judicially scored, and the design upon which its rhythm is constructed is both ingenious and original'.

The bi-centenary concert held in September 1970 in St

[7] *Musical Times*, May, 1970.

THE GUILDHALL BUILT BY TROLLAP IN 1658

THE GUILDHALL AFTER THE ADDITION OF A CLASSICAL FRONT BY DAVID STEPHENSON IN 1796

CAPHEATON HALL

ROBERT CROSSBY'S PAINTING OF CAPHEATON HALL
(by courtesy of Mr John Browne-Swinburne
and the University of Newcastle upon Tyne)

(Oriel Press)

CAPHEATON HALL, EAST DOORWAY

(Country Life)

CAPHEATON HALL, SOUTH DOORWAY

BOCKENFIELD MANOR HOUSE (Oriel Press)

(Oriel Press)

SWARLAND OLD HALL

(Country Life)

CALLALY CASTLE, THE ENTRANCE FRONT

CHARLES AVISON
A portrait by an unknown artist
(by courtesy of the Provost and Chapter of St Nicholas' Cathedral)

THOMAS BEWICK
(from a portrait by James Ramsay)

Northumberland Bank

No. _____

No. _____

I promise to pay the Bearer on demand ONE POUND, Value rec.d

Newcastle _____ 18

For Sir Francis Blake Bar.t

John Reed, Reeds & Co.

One Pound

Ent.d d Yorke Watson

Bewick

A BANK NOTE DESIGNED BY BEWICK

THOMAS BEWICK. TAILPIECES

THOMAS BEWICK. TAILPIECES

THOMAS BEWICK. TRADE ENGRAVINGS

(Victoria and Albert Museum)
BEILBY GLASS

(Victoria and Albert Museum)
BEILBY GLASS

Nicholas Cathedral showed what a gift for limpid and elegiac melody he possessed, and made one regret that only a few of his works are still available on records. In particular his Concerto in E Minor (Op. 6, No. 8) has, as part of the second movement, a melody which does not soar but rises gently and seems about to fall beyond recall when miraculously it is caught again and again. It may not be a purely musical appreciation, and may be as much indicative of an affection for Georgian Newcastle as for Georgian music, but whenever I walk past St Andrew's Churchyard where since May 1770 Charles Avison has lain, that melody seems to me to speak for him with a sadness unsurpassed by any other.

CHAPTER THREE

Thomas Bewick and the Beilby Family

WHEN William Beilby senior (1706-1765), a silversmith and jeweller born in Scarborough, failed in business in Durham and came to Gateshead to make a fresh start, dying there in 1765, he would have been surprised to learn that a difficult and unsuccessful life had won him a permanent place in the history of English Decorative Art. For whilst all his seven children (five sons and two daughters) inherited their father's love of art, five of them excelled in its practice in widely varying forms, and two—William and Mary—were to win particular and growing recognition.

Richard, the eldest son who died in his thirties before 1767, served an apprenticeship as a seal engraver in Birmingham; William, the second son (1740-1819) learnt painting and enamelling also in Birmingham, that town being then with Bilston and London the centre of the art of making and decorating enamel objects. William taught the art to his younger brother Thomas (who later opened a school for drawing in Leeds) and also to his younger sister Mary (1749-1797); Ralph (1743-1817) for a short time adopted his father's trade as a silversmith, his lifelong love was music (he was always on terms of close friendship with Charles Avison's two sons) but he early became an engraver. He will always be remembered for the fact that on 1st October, 1767, when he was only twenty-four years of age, he took as his apprentice the then fourteen-year-old Thomas Bewick. The Beilby family, although holding a semi-artistic status by virtue of their various trades, would in their day have been beneath serious social acknowledgement by anyone considering himself a member of polite society (unless he was an exceptionally intelligent member of that society), but their influence on the artistic life of Newcastle was to be both profound and long-lasting.

After the death of the father in 1765, the mother assisted by the two daughters (Mary would then only be sixteen), in an attempt to support themselves, opened a school in Gateshead; but the trial at Assizes of Jameson, the Newcastle engraver, for forgery, although resulting in Jameson's acquittal, resulted in him also leaving the town, and presented a sudden opportunity to Ralph Beilby to move to Newcastle where he opened up an engraving business and with the help of the whole family—some working in the business and others keeping house for him—he soon built up a successful business at Amen Corner, facing St Nicholas' Churchyard where Bewick was to join him in 1767.

It is William and Mary Beilby who are now famous as the artists who painted in enamel on glass and whose work is now so sought after, but it is obvious from what happened later that like the plasterers and stone carvers working for Trollap, they had no very grandiose conception of their work but thought of themselves merely as craftsmen in a trade.

Bewick records in his Memoir—

'... such was the industry of my master that he refused nothing, coarse or fine. He undertook everything ... fitted up and tempered his own tools and adapted them to every purpose ... This readiness brought him in an overflow of work, and the workplace was filled with the coarsest kind of steel stamps, pipe moulds, bottle moulds, brass clock faces, door plates, coffin plates, bookbinders, letters and stamps, steel, silver and gold seals, mourning rings etc. He also undertook the engraving of arms, crests and cyphers on silver and every kind of job from the silversmiths; also engraving bills of exchange, banknotes, invoices, account-heads, and cards ... but what he excelled in was ornamental silver engraving. In this, as far as I am able to judge he was one of the best in the kingdom.'

When Bewick joined the Beilby family in 1767 as an apprentice, William would be aged twenty-seven years, and Mary about eighteen, and Bewick records they 'had constant employment of enamel-painting of glass'. Ralph Beilby has been described as a wood engraver but he did very little of it, did it badly, and disliked what he did, so that when any such work came in, it was given to young Bewick who quickly became most skilled at it. With the services of Bewick therefore, the firm was able to undertake work of wood engraving which otherwise it could not have done, and Ralph Beilby was able to pursue with less interruption his special aptitude for engraving on silver, and so the firm of Beilby prospered.

Bewick in his Memoir writes of his falling in love with Mary Beilby:

> 'I had formed a strong attachment to her but could not make this known to her or to anyone else ... I pined and fretted at so many bars in the way of our union. One of the greatest was the supposed contempt in which I was held by the rest of the family, who, I thought treated me with great hauteur, though I had done everything in my power to oblige them. I had, like a stable boy waited upon their horse; and had cheerfully done everything they wanted at my hands till one of the brothers grossly affronted me in the business of the stable. This I instantly resented and refused attendance there any more. Before I was out of my time, Miss Beilby had a paralytic stroke which very greatly altered her looks and rendered her for some time unhappy. Long after this she went with her eldest brother into Fifeshire where she died.'

After the termination of his indentures on 1st October, 1774, Bewick had a year or two away from any regular employment and made a walking tour of Scotland, and on his return cut blocks when and for whom he pleased, went fishing in the Tyne Valley, and then decided to go to London to improve his knowledge of art in general and of wood engraving in particular. As a disciple of William Cobbett and a confirmed countryman even then in his likes and dislikes, it is not surprising that he got on well neither with London nor its people. 'I would even enlist for a soldier or go and herd sheep at five shillings per week as long as I lived, rather than be tied to live in London'—and he returned in 1777, after nearly a year away from Tyneside to find that his old master Ralph Beilby was offering him a partnership in his business. Even at that stage, Ralph, a keen businessman and the real head of the Beilby family, taking precedence over the older and more artistic William, must have recognized and been willing to pay a price to harness, what he regarded as an exceptional talent. Bewick accepted, and took in his younger brother John to serve as an apprentice under him.

It was the very next year (1778) that old Mrs Beilby died, and William and Mary Beilby left to live in Fifeshire and enamelled on glass no more; 'It is significant that painting by the Beilbys has not yet been found on several types of glass which came into vogue in the last quarter of the century.'[1]

It is not yet known why William and Mary Beilby left the firm of Beilby in 1778. The death of old Mrs Beilby provides no discernible reason why they should leave the firm and give up their painting, and it seems more likely that Bewick's coming into partnership only one year earlier had unsettled William and Mary, or had given rise to some dissension which would help to explain their otherwise surprising departure. There was to be contention and bitterness exactly twenty years later in 1797 when Ralph Beilby dissolved his partnership with Bewick. Bewick in his autobiography says a good deal about how he and Ralph Beilby dissolved partnership but gives no reason whatsoever for the departure of William and Mary in 1778—which seems strange. One is struck by the great probability that the pleasure given to generations by Bewick's designs and vignettes was at the price of the Beilbys' premature withdrawal from their enamel painting on glass. There is also something that needs explaining too from the point of view of the prospering Ralph, in that it must be unusual by any standards to allow a situation to develop in which an older brother and an invalid sister, leave not only the brother's flourishing business but the family circle as well. However—although English decorative art lost much by William and Mary's disappearance—it is doubtful if they suffered poverty; William went from Fife to Battersea in 1784, opened a school, prospered, and married a wealthy woman who bought a great estate in Fife which William managed. There seems to

[1] 'The Beilby Glasses' by W. A. Thorpe, *The Connoisseur*, May 1928, page 19, an invaluable article.

be no evidence that Mary ever left Fifeshire after going there in 1778 and her sad story ends with her death in only her forty-ninth year in 1797.

Richard Beilby, the eldest son, had died before Bewick's 1767 apprenticeship to Ralph; William was three years older than Ralph, and Mary six years younger than Ralph. The earliest dateable Beilby enamelling on glass is the glass (illustrated) decorated with the Prince of Wales' Feathers and the Royal Arms of King George III. This glass celebrates the birth of a Prince of Wales in 1762 and is a Beilby signed glass. This earliest known glass was therefore painted by William when he was only twenty-two years of age and at a time when Mary was only thirteen. This Beilby glass was painted five years before Bewick was apprenticed to the Beilby firm, and since Ralph only moved to Amen Corner at St Nicholas' Churchyard, Newcastle, after his father's death in 1765, then the earlier Beilby painted glasses must have been enamel-painted in Gateshead. But the most extraordinary fact in the history of the Beilby family, is that there is no trace of the celebrated Beilby enamel painting on glass outside the period 1762-1778—i.e. for a period of sixteen years only—and that, having retired to Fife, William and Mary never enamelled another glass in their lives! So that they must not have believed (as posterity does) that there was anything of particular merit and importance in their work.

I have referred to enamelling by William and Mary. In fact when they retired to Fife in 1778 Mary would only be twenty-nine years of age. Since she was only thirteen when the enamel painting began in 1762, and since in her early twenties she suffered a stroke which left her an invalid and partly paralysed, the amount of enamelling done by her must have been limited. It is not possible to distinguish any difference in style in the various paintings on the glasses and the rare signature is merely the surname 'Beilby' or 'Beilby Junr' in what appears to be the same style of writing. Although it is obvious from what Bewick says in his Autobiography that she did some of the decorative enamelling, it is equally obvious that the credit for the vast majority of the painting must go to William.

There have of course been other enamellers on glass—Michael Edkins of Bristol who could decorate anything from coaches to porcelain, and William Absolon of Great Yarmouth, are only two of several. But no painter on glass has been able to equal the delicacy and elegance of the Beilbys' painting. Their 'white' enamel has a bluish and sometimes a pinkish tinge which is pleasing and their rare work in coloured enamels is so highly prized that it will today cost well over two thousand pounds to secure a good example. Some of their landscape scenes on glass have a detail and character that is strangely reminiscent of some of Bewick's vignettes. These were almost certainly late works and because Ralph, as a well known engraver on silver would be used to engraving coats of arms on silver, it is not surprising that the earliest Beilby glasses that can be dated, are decorated with coats of arms and heraldic forms on which no doubt the older Ralph could give William good advice to ensure accuracy.

Later, they painted the leaf and vine and grape and hop designs, which were to a great extent merely repeating in enamel paint the older designs which had been already engraved by the glass engravers. But later came the charming landscapes with buildings, sometimes classical and sometimes Chinese, and ruins and obelisks, and rural scenes—sheep in a landscape or country sports and pastimes—all achieving a surprising vitality and character and depth on an inch or so of glass.

The Beilby painting was all done—with extremely rare exceptions—on Newcastle glass, that is to say on glasses manufactured in the glasshouses of this area. This Newcastle glass ranked in the eighteenth century with the finest glass from Ireland, London and Bristol, as the best glass in Western Europe, partly due to flint glass having been made in Newcastle from as early as 1684 by the Dagnia brothers, and from 1728 by Joseph Airey whose firm later became, Airey, Cookson and Company. These were the only two flint-glass companies operating in Newcastle until 1782, and each did an enormous trade exporting to Europe. So great was the reputation of Newcastle glass that by the middle of the eighteenth century famous Dutch engravers such as David Wolff and Aert Schouman did their engraving on Newcastle glasses, whilst research[2] has also shown that most of the so-called Jacobite glasses carrying inscriptions supporting the House

[2] See the article by W. A. Thorpe 'The Dagnia Tradition in Newcastle Glass', *The Connoisseur*, July, 1933, page 13.

of Stuart were made in Newcastle.

Although therefore in 1778 William and Mary had disappeared somewhat mysteriously into Fifeshire, Ralph Beilby remained in partnership with Bewick for another nineteen years. Perhaps it is surprising that the partnership lasted as long as it did since they were both strong minded artisan artists with a good sense of their own worth, men of independent spirit who usually insisted on getting their own way.

In 1785 Bewick commenced to engrave the blocks for the famous *History of Quadrupeds* for which Ralph Beilby wrote the text. Published in 1790 when Bewick was thirty-seven years old, the book was a tremendous success, Bewick's wood engravings and vignettes representing an advance on any previous engraving work for book publication in sharpness of detail and in story telling within a minute space. At this time engraving on copper was the usual method for illustrating and decorating books, it having entirely superseded engraving on wood which was then regarded merely as an antique German practice—until Bewick's work brought about its revival. The first Land Bird volume of the *History of British Birds*, again with text by Ralph Beilby and wood engravings by Bewick, came out in 1797 (the years the partnership ended) and was again, a great success. But the second volume describing the water birds did not come out until 1804 (in which book Bewick wrote the text himself), by which time the partnership had been dissolved for seven years, Bewick was in business on his own, and Ralph Beilby had left engraving behind him for ever, to develop his partnership interest in a successful firm of watch-glass and clock manufacturers which eventually built new premises and carried on business in Orchard Street until Ralph Beilby retired.

There is nearly always an element of the comic about other people's quarrels although, of course, never about our own; and the dispute which led to the dissolution of the partnership had that element and, in addition, a certain pathos. One feels that the real roots of the quarrel lie deep in other dissensions, and that Bewick's behaviour reflected a resentment harboured for nearly thirty years at the 'supposed contempt' with which he considered he had been treated by some members of the Beilby family during his apprenticeship. But the quarrel which occasioned the dissolution had its immediate origin in Beilby's jealousy of Bewick's growing fame following upon the publication of the Quadrupeds in 1790, his own wish for some literary recognition, and Bewick's stubborn nature, which refused to concede Beilby's reasonable demand that the work he had done in writing the text for The Quadrupeds and for the Land Birds in 1797 should be more plainly stated in the books.

On the title page of *A General History of Quadrupeds* immediately under the title and plain for all the world to see in large letters it is proclaimed, 'The Figures engraved on wood by T. BEWICK'. There is no mention of the name of the main author of the text, yet the advertisement which served as a preface to the book did by the use of the plural throughout, e.g. 'We have endeavoured to lay before our readers ...' indicate that others in addition to Bewick were entitled to credit for the production. In very small letters at the foot of the page are the words 'Printed by and for S. Hodgson, R. Beilby and T. Bewick'. Hodgson was the printer and publisher of the book who, for his services, had been granted a third share of the book; it was therefore just possible for the careful reader, by inference, to work out for himself that Beilby was entitled to some credit for the text—but it is not surprising that Beilby felt his work less than adequately recognized.

Bewick records in his Memoir that Beilby was so aggrieved that—

'... while the title page was in hand, Mr Beilby wished to be made the author of it and wrote in his name as such "by R. Beilby". On Mr Hodgson seeing this, without saying a word he stroked the name out with a pen, while Mr Beilby was looking on. I knew nothing of this transaction for some time afterwards ...'

Beilby therefore lost the first round. But in 1797 when Beilby wrote the text for the first volume of the *History of British Birds* (assisted and frequently corrected by Bewick when difficult points arose), he pursued a much more subtle line of attack which angered Bewick. In his Memoir Bewick wrote—

'Mr Beilby undertook the writing or compilation of this

(the first) volume in which I assisted him a great deal more than I had done with the Quadrupeds. I was however surprised to find that in an Introduction written by him he took occasion to bestow the most unqualified praises on me for the assistance I had given him, by which I found he was this time determined upon being an author. I only observed that I thought the Quadrupeds with the title of "Beilby and Bewick" as the Editors,[3] had done very well and I could see no reason for making any change ... In this unsettled state of affairs Mr and Mrs Beilby set off in the pet upon a visit ... where they remained about a fortnight. On Mr Beilby's return I asked him if he still persisted in being named as the author of the book to which he replied in the affirmative.'

Bewick therefore proposed, and Beilby accepted, that a committee of their mutual friends acting as referees should decide the point as to whether Beilby should have his name as author on the title page. So Emmerson Charnley, the bookseller, The Reverend William Turner, Secretary of the Newcastle Literary and Philosophical Society, Mr Sol Hodgson (who had no share in the new work), and Mr George Doubleday, met together in the afternoon, the disputants set out their cases in writing to the President (Mr Charnley), who handed the written documents round for study, and the Committee then retired to make their somewhat surprising decision which, as Bewick writes with satisfaction in his Memoir—'they committed what they had agreed upon to writing, the whole of which was printed in the concluding part of the preface to the first Volume of the Birds, and so the matter was left without naming either him or myself as authors of the work, otherwise as before, and of the wood-cuts being acknowledged as my own. After this Mr Beilby gave up the engraving business ...'

So Beilby was defeated in his second attempt to have his name mentioned on the title page of the book as author of the text, and one feels that Bewick with his name again on the title page—'THE FIGURES ENGRAVED ON WOOD BY T. BEWICK'—should have been more generous. The formula agreed upon by the Committee

[3] This is inaccurate for although it is inferentially discernible there is no express mention of the name of Beilby as Editor in the quadrupeds.

of friends and to be read in the Preface is in the following words—'It may be proper to observe, that while one of the editors of this work was engaged in preparing the engravings, the compilation of the descriptions was undertaken by the other, subject however to the corrections of his friend whose habits had led him to a more intimate acquaintance with this branch of Natural History'. Nowhere in the book is it stated that the name of the chief compiler of the text is Ralph Beilby, except by inference to be drawn from the above and from the announcement that it is 'Printed by Sol Hodgson for Beilby and Bewick'—the only express mention of Beilby's name in the book.

Bewick's robust view was that the text was nothing and his engravings everything. That is certainly posterity's view; but Bewick's view that without his engravings the text was unsaleable, whilst without the text the engravings would sell by themselves, was not proved correct. When with Beilby's consent (for they subsequently maintained an outwardly correct if distant relationship) the engravings were published without the text 'for R. Beilby and T. Bewick' in 1800, under the title of *Figures of British Land Birds*, so few copies were sold that the great majority were destroyed.

So ended on a sour note Bewick's thirty-year association with the Beilby family. And Bewick writes of Beilby's exacted price from him of £100 for Beilby's third share of the Quadrupeds and £300 for his half share of the Birds—'I could not help thinking he had suffered greediness to take possession of his mind ... I had noticed for some time past, that he had been led under a guidance and influence that made an alteration in his conduct and character for the worse; and he appeared to me not to be the Ralph Beilby he had been.'

But nearly all human characters and motives are difficult to assess. It is the same Beilby insisting on a price of £100 and £300 (which Bewick could ill afford) as the price of his share in the two books, when he knew that Bewick had in each case spent years on the preparation of the wood cuts constituting the book's only real claim to fame, who had yet in 1777 invited Bewick to become a partner in his flourishing and established business without asking for anything in return. Part of the truth is that as Beilby grew older he sought increasing public regard and acceptance as a gentleman—and would therefore particularly prize the name of author which Bewick denied him. His religiosity increased; his desire for money increased; and he became one of those who down the ages like Johnson's Richard Savage, have mistaken 'the Love of for the Practice of Virtue'.

Bewick's daughter Jane (a biased witness) says[4] that her father would not see that Beilby was a cunning man until it was too late, that his Pecksniffian letters paint his character, that his wife and he 'assumed to be very genteel people' and that he was full of pretension. The tragedy ended with Bewick going to see him in 1817 when Beilby was on his death bed; Mrs Beilby refused him entry, although Bewick from the stairs heard Beilby say to his wife 'I *will* see him.' Bewick was not invited and did not attend the funeral of his old master.

Although as artist-tradesmen, Beilby and Bewick had much in common, their personalities increasingly diverged as the years went by. Bewick never acted up to his increasing renown. He remained his natural radical Cobbett-like self and, if anything, acted down to it—refusing (like T. M. Richardson) to moderate in any way his broad Tyneside dialect, enclosing his massive frame in loose rough clothes, and in later years carrying a stick that was more like a cudgel; but the whole picture he presented was relieved by the intelligence and liveliness of his wit and expression. This man who after the age of twenty-four was compelled to spend most of his life over the bench in his workshop looked like what he most admired—'there is no business of any kind that can be compared to that of a man who farms his own land. It appears to me that every earthly pleasure is within his reach.' In essence, Bewick remained rooted in the mid-eighteenth century, and Beilby, in advance of the times, became a pattern for what was to be the early Victorian Age.

With increasing fame (one can never say wealth, because Bewick died worth less than £2,000) Bewick never abated his hatred of all war in general, or his opposition to the 'war for despotism' against France in particular. His loathing for Pitt, his dislike of dictatorship whether monarchical or otherwise, his

---

[4] This manuscript written by Jane Bewick in 1861 is in the Laing Art Gallery, Newcastle, and I am grateful to the Laing Art Gallery and to Mr Iain Bain for allowing me to have sight of extracts from it.

distrust of nearly all who wield power in society, his dislike of religious enthusiasm and intolerance—whether of the old kind or of the Methodists of his own day are all vigorously expressed in the Memoir of his life. These radical sentiments coming from a man who was winning increasing recognition from the world, and who plainly did not set over-much store by it, would lend impressive weight to his words in the political debates at Swarley's Club at the Black Boy in the Groat Market, and in discussions with his many friends and acquaintances at his other favourite inns where, 'I frequently, by way of unbending the mind after the labours of the day, spent my evenings chiefly at the Blue Bell in company with a set of staunch advocates for the liberties of mankind who discussed the passing events mostly with the cool, sensible, and deliberate attention which the importance of the subject required ... men of sense and consequence in Newcastle', and at the Unicorn with 'mostly tradesmen of the genteel sort'. The more formal debates at Swarley's Club were later abandoned for fear of being noticed by Government spies and agents.

Bewick was a thorough patriot with a profound belief in the ordinary English people—the more simple and ordinary they were (such as the labourers of the Tyne Valley amongst whom he had spent his childhood), the more he respected them and did them honour. He was a highly religious man who hated religiosity. His religion was based on a passionate love of the Creation, and of all Nature. The Memoir which he wrote in the 1820s for his daughter Jane and which she would not allow to be published until 1862, is second only to Benjamin Haydon's diary in the revealing of an artist as a whole man. Like Haydon, Bewick was utterly uncompromising in his views and attitude to life and a great many of his quarrels (and there were many) and his difficulties with apprentices and others sprang from this. But neither his essentially puritan view of life, nor his impatient indignation, nor the morbid side to his nature (hinted at in some of the vignettes), prevented him being for most of the time a man who loved the company of his fellow men.

It is unfortunate that the Memoir was not published until Victorian values were firmly established. The Memoir has been much scolded by former editors and commentators who, paying tribute to the wonderful picture it drew of a boy growing up in the eighteenth century in the then paradise of the Tyne Valley, and for its vivid word pictures, have deplored the 'preaching and the moralizing', and the political radicalism which the Reverend Hugo, Jane Bewick, Austin Dobson, and Julia Boyd plainly viewed as an unfortunate aberration. A careful reading today induces a quite different response to a man who in his reverence for life and freedom was far ahead of his time—indeed of all time.

This reaction of unease and embarrassment to parts of the Memoir arose from such scathing passages as on his experience in reading 'the chaos of what is called religious works'. 'I got myself into a labyrinth bewildered with dogmas, creeds and opinions, mostly the fanatical reveries or the bigoted inventions of interested or designing men that seemed to me without end.' He reflects that 'Wagon loads of sermons have been published— some of them perhaps good—in order to prove matters (in my opinion) of no importance to religion or morality ... The beauty and simplicity of the doctrines laid down by the inspired and benevolent Author of the Christian religion, however they may have been distorted and disfigured, are yet in themselves perfect.' After discussing the differing sects from Catholic to Quaker he concludes, 'Whatever the creed may be there can be no objection to the religion of a virtuous man; and it is to be hoped ... that the bickerings ... will cease, and the causes of them be thought of no more importance than whether a man uses his quid of tobacco in the right cheek or the left.'

He cast a critical eye at landowners. 'Gentlemen should endeavour to improve their lands and lay the foundation of fertilizing them, and instead of spending—perhaps squandering—their monies in follies abroad, as far as possible, spend it at home. I cannot help thinking that if the same pains were taken in breeding mankind that gentlemen have bestowed upon the breeding of horses and dogs, human nature might, as it were, be new modelled, hereditary diseases banished.' On the Game Laws he wrote 'To convince the intelligent poor man that the fowls of the air were created only for the rich is impossible, and will ever remain so'. On Pitt and the French Wars he exploded, 'Knaves and their abettors appeared to predominate in the land; and they carried their subserviency to such a length that I think if

Mr Pitt had proposed to make a law to transport all men who had pug noses, and to hang all men above sixty years of age, these persons (those excepted who came within the Act) would have advocated it as a brilliant thought and a wise measure'.

His reverence for life and nature made him all the more conscious of death. This aspect of him shows frequently in his engravings and even as a life long angler, passionately devoted to the sport, he was troubled and reflected that he 'ought not totally to forget that what is sport to him is death to them'. On hunting he was ahead of his time and ours:

'The pursuing, baiting or killing these animals, never at that time struck me as cruel. The mind had not as yet been impressed with the feelings of humanity. This, however, came upon me at last; and the first time I felt the change happened by my having (in hunting) caught the hare in my arms, while surrounded by the dogs and the hunters, when the poor terrified creature screamed out so piteously—like a child—that I would have given anything to have saved its life. In this however I was prevented; for a farmer well known to me who stood close by, pressed upon me, and desired I would "give her to him"; and, from his being better able (as I thought) to save its life, I complied with his wish. This was no sooner done than he proposed to those about him, "to have a bit more sport with her", and this was to be done by breaking one of its legs, and then again setting the poor animal off a little before the dogs. I wandered away to a little distance, oppressed by my own feelings and could not join the crew again ...'

He loved the land and the people on it, and was as much angered by the Enclosure Acts driving the peasants into the towns as by the extravagance and pride of the gentry resulting in them 'sliding away into nothingness, and ... to see their mansions mouldering away'. Appalled at the prostitution and degradation in London existing side by side with great wealth and grandeur, he loved the Highlander for having neither. Courteous to all who were courteous to him he never took off his hat to anybody for long. When the gentry and the great called upon him at his workshop, where he sat working always with his brown silk cap

(Victoria and Albert Museum)
BEILBY GLASS

(Royal Scottish Museum, Edinburgh)
BEILBY GLASS

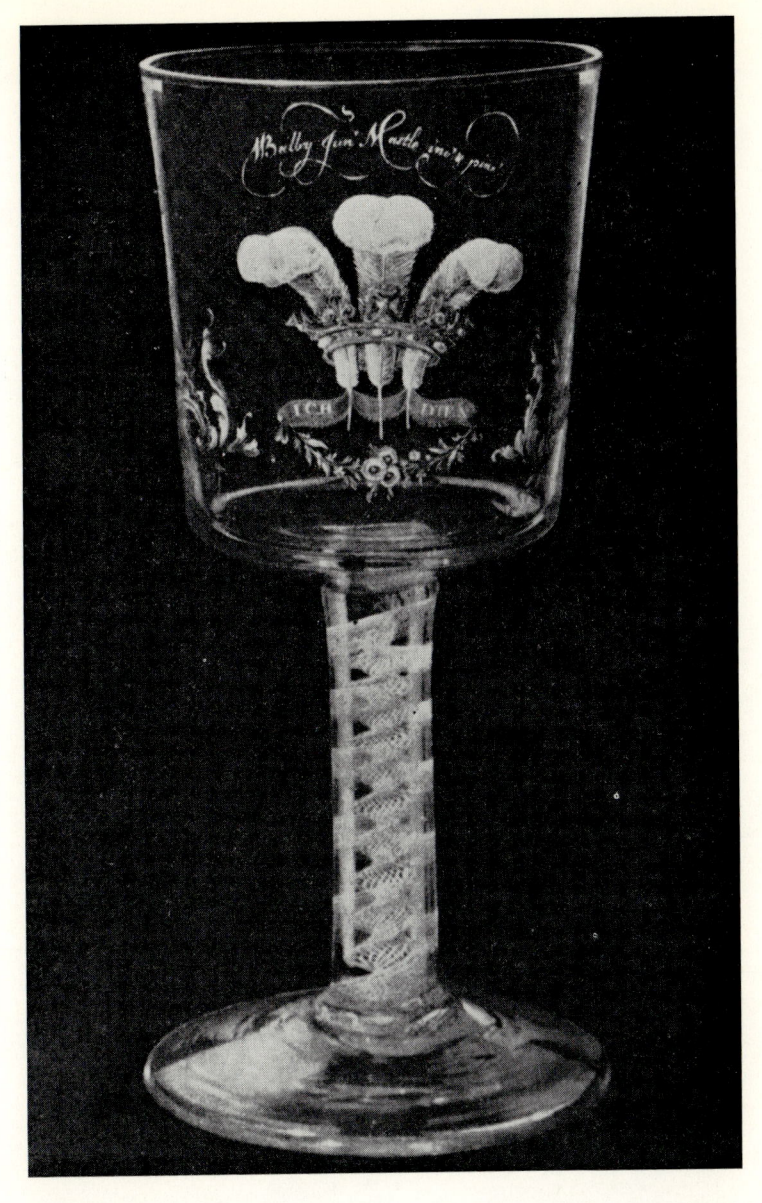

(photograph G. Cockburn)
SIGNED BEILBY GLASS CELEBRATING BIRTH OF PRINCE OF WALES, 1762

The MARGARET and WINNEFORD

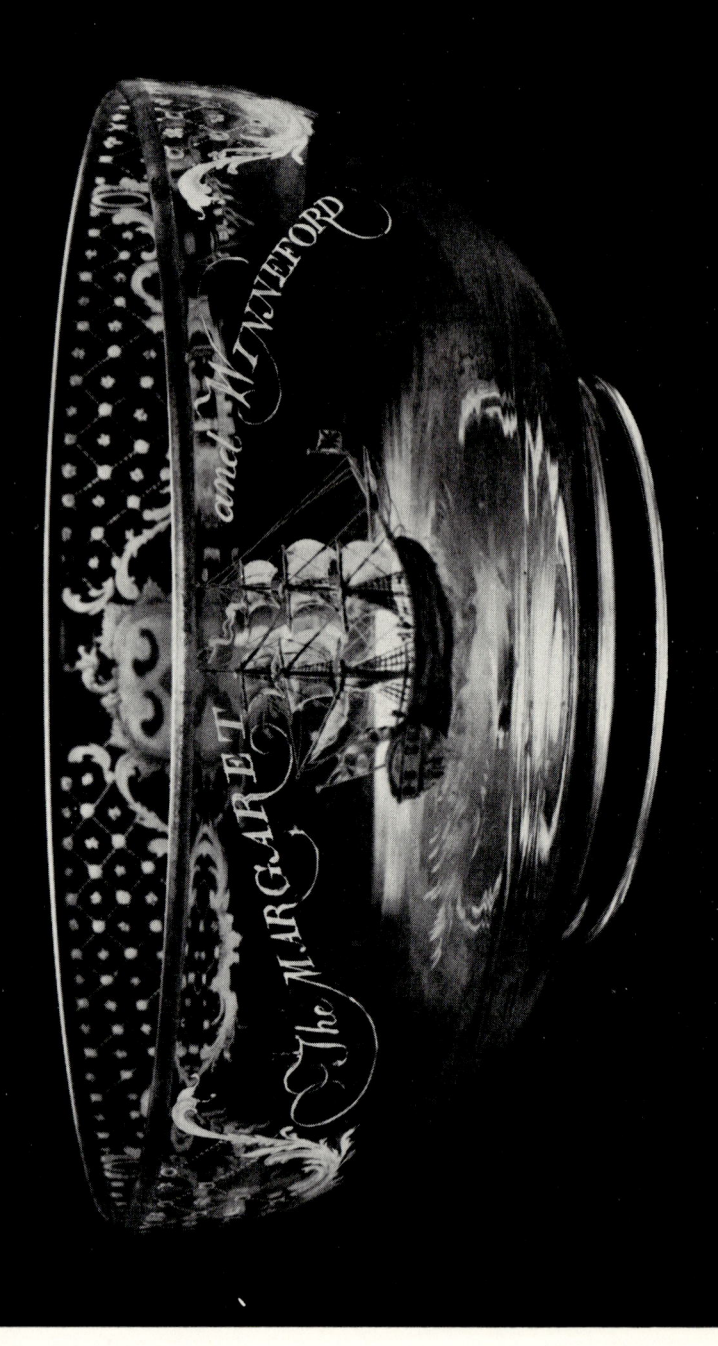

T. M. Richardson, senior (Laing Art Gallery)

NEWCASTLE FROM GATESHEAD FELL
T. M. RICHARDSON (SENIOR)

(Laing Art Gallery)

EVENING ON THE TYNE BY T. M. RICHARDSON
(Watercolour)
(G. Cockburn)

GRAINGER STREET BY T. M. RICHARDSON (Laing Art Gallery)

LION BRIDGE, ALNWICK BY T. M. RICHARDSON
(Watercolour)
(Laing Art Gallery)

RICHARD GRAINGER, 1797-1861

(Oriel Press)

THE BANK OF ENGLAND BUILT BY GRAINGER, PROBABLY DESIGNED BY JOHN WARDLE

(Oriel Pr

THE THEATRE ROYAL BUILT BY GRAINGER AND DESIGNED BY
JOHN AND BENJAMIN GREEN

UPPER GREY STREET SHOWING LLOYDS BANK BUILDING AND THEATRE ROYAL PORTICO

(Oriel Press)

UPPER GREY STREET SHOWING TWO OF THE THREE DOMES OF THE CENTRAL EXCHANGE

GREY STREET (Engraving)

LONGHIRST HALL BY JOHN DOBSON, 1828.

on, he would remove it from his head momentarily as a sign that he had noted their entry but would replace it at once.

A rural conservative, although a radical in politics, he showed foresight in distrusting the beginning of the more intensive agriculture and the higher returns sought from it—an insidious process which today if unchecked threatens to destroy soil, hedge, plant and animal life and ourselves. 'This was before the pernicious use of chemical compounds was known, or agricultural improvements had quickened the eyes of landlords, banished many small farmers, soured their countenances, and altered for the worse the characters of the larger ones that remained ...'

But it is as a description of a boy's growing-up in the Tyne Valley countryside of the mid-eighteenth century, and of the characters who lived there, that the Memoir ranks as one of the best autobiographies in the English language. There is in the book the same fear of the night and of the dead as in the engravings, and the same consciousness of cruelty and of life hurrying by. And in his old age, towards the end of the Memoir, he speaks his thoughts as he waits for death like his skeletal horse (Bewick met it first), 'I might name others of the like character, but they have left this world long ago ... and thus noticing them puts me in mind of its being like creeping out of this world ... Some men from the first, as soon as they die are quite unnoticed—some are remembered only for a day and some a little while longer ... and the numbers of both the one and the other appeared to me to be so immense ... like attempting to count the grains of sand on the sea beach. It is thus that the grave swallows up all without distinction.'

Bewick's engravings on the wood were not only the most vivid expression of his love of nature, but also showed a feeling for composition and a passion crossing the line that divides craft from art. It is not only that the plumage of the bird exceeds anything previously shown on wood or copper plate engraving, but the landscape in which the bird is shown and the relationship between branch and bird rivals anything achieved in any other medium. Ruskin in his 'Elements of Drawing' called Bewick 'The Burns of Painting'. Wordsworth who shared with Bewick (and with Ruskin) the same obsessive passion for particularity of detail—in stone, in leaf, in flower, in feather—sang Bewick's praise in verse almost as execrable as that in which the anonymous versifier sang Trollap's —

'O now that the genius of Bewick were mine,
And the skill which he learned on the Banks of the Tyne
Then the Muses might deal with me just as they chose,
For I'd take my last leave both of verse and of prose'

Julia Boyd[5] quotes Ruskin's assertion in Ariadne Florentina (1876), the text of the lectures he had delivered in Oxford in 1872: 'I know no drawing so subtle as Bewick's since the fifteenth century, except Holbein's and Turner's', and Montague Weekley in his Biography[6] quotes another Ruskin assessment of Bewick, '... the precision of his unerring hand—his inevitable eye—and his rightly judging heart—should place him in the first rank of the great artists not of England only, but of all the world and of all time'.

Bewick, the greatest nature teacher and illustrator of his age, unlike Gilbert White, lived nearly all of his life, to his sorrow, in a town. Moreover, the works for which he is famous today were the mere by-product of an extremely busy life—work done in the evening at the end of a day spent in doing the sort of work on which he relied to make his living—designing and engraving on silver, copper plate or wood engraving for cheques, bill heads, trade and invitation cards, or for a great variety of other everyday things. This work has often an elegance reflecting the best in eighteenth-century design, and shows us that his 'jobbing' can be just as beautiful as his book illustrations.

Some of his best work is first to be found in the 1784 edition of *Select Fables* published by Bewick's first patron of any consequence, the Newcastle bookseller, Thomas Saint. This is a truly delightful book containing some engravings by Bewick's younger brother John who, had he lived beyond the age of thirty-five, would probably have equalled Bewick's own achievement. There had been a 1776 edition of *Select Fables*, also published by Saint, but the engravings illustrating the first two-thirds

---
[5] Her introduction to 'Bewick Gleanings' 1886.
[6] at page 192.

of the book are so poor that there must be grave doubt whether they are Bewick's, even allowing for the fact that he would be then only twenty-three years old. There is a copper plate engraving by Ralph Beilby as a frontispiece to this book. In the last third of this book, 'Fables in Verse', the standard of the oval wood engravings is immensely better, and those on pages 180 and 193 are extremely fine. In the 1784 edition all the cuts from the first two-thirds of the book are omitted, and are replaced by work as good as anything that Thomas or John Bewick ever achieved in their lives.

In the 1790 Quadrupeds, the stiffness and lack of conviction in some of the engravings is due to the fact that Bewick had not seen live specimens of some of the animals—but the vignettes are always a delight. In the Land Birds of 1797 and in the Water Birds of 1804, both the birds and the vignettes are equally delectable—and these two books constitute Bewick's master-work, culminating in the 1826 edition which is the last edition Bewick himself revised and which contains a number of additional birds and tail-pieces. But Thomas Bewick's illustrations to *Poems by Goldsmith and Parnell* published by William Bulmer in 1795 (the year of John Bewick's death) and the same publisher's production of Somerville's 'Chase', of 1796, in which the cuts were nearly all by John Bewick but were finished off by the elder Bewick after John's death, are also very fine; and there is plenty to admire in Bewick's woodcuts illustrating Bishop Percy's *Hermit of Warkworth* published by John Catnach of Alnwick in 1805 and in Bewick's last complete work, the illustrations to *Aesop's Fables* published in 1818.

Bewick's work founded a new school of English Wood-Engraving. His pupils were active after his death and such wood engravers as Joan Hassall, Gwen Raverat, Robert Gibbings, Reynolds Stone and George Mackley have carried on the Bewick tradition into the present day.

Bewick died at his home at 19 West Street, Gateshead, on 8th November, 1828, at a time when he was working with his son Robert Elliot Bewick on a proposed *History of Fishes* for which Bewick had completed all the tailpieces. The present Post Office building stands on the site of the house in which he died. His workshop in St Nicholas' Churchyard was still surviving in

1886 when Julia Boyd wrote her Introduction but is now demolished; but the wood blocks, the water colours, the prose writings, and the books themselves are beyond destruction so long as a literate civilization survives.

CHAPTER FOUR

Thomas Miles Richardson (Senior)

F E W sights are more dispiriting than the average English Watercolour. As the nineteenth century advanced, increasingly watery and prettified products vied with highly accented body-coloured scenes, often by artists of great technical ability, eventually reaching a point beyond recall as works of art. And because these are the only kind of watercolours that are seen in their hundreds each year in salerooms and galleries, unless one is lucky enough to be brought by chance to a watercolour by one of the eighteenth-century masters or an early nineteenth-century watercolour by (say) Lear or Shotter Boys, these are the only kind of watercolours most people are ever likely to know.

But of course the Galleries specializing in early English Watercolours tell a very different story. And further investigation from the earliest drawings of Francis Place and Barlow through the rich achievement of the eighteenth century to the early years of the nineteenth, opens up a whole new world of delight and delicacy. Even in the years of the decline of the watercolour, many artists still remained constant to the old tradition of truth, topography, and subtle colouring, ignoring the public demand for sentiment and lurid colour; William Callow, Thomas Churchyard, J. D. Harding, Luke Clennell, William Havell, William Turner of Oxford, are only a very few of these many who continued to supplement the heights scaled by Turner, J. R. Cozens and the Shoreham Palmer with admirable work; and in any list of those artists who continued to work in the old tradition until the middle of the nineteenth century there should be mentioned the name of Thomas Miles Richardson (Senior) born in Newcastle on 15th May, 1784.

In the most recent authoritative work on English Watercolours[1] Martin Hardie mentions some—

> 'minor artists ... with some passage of skill and liveliness to be found in their work. That is true of the work of Thomas Miles Richardson, father and son, W. L. Leitch and their group who anticipated the crude ideals of the coloured picture post-card in their sentimentalized version of nature.'

This linking of the elder Richardson with his son (T. M. Richardson, Junior) and Leitch in sentimentalizing nature is entirely wrong. The elder Richardson never sentimentalized anything in any picture I have seen. Martin Hardie continues wrongly to link the two together—

> 'The Richardsons knew all the tricks for certain definite effects to be gained by a free use of body-colour, often garish and over-accented.'

The truth is that even in some galleries in London I have seen the works of the son attributed to the father, and everything that Martin Hardie says is true of the son who, although the author of some beautiful water-colours in his early years (many of Northumbrian scenes), had the artistic misfortune to outlive his father into a time when the new middle classes were discovering the Mediterranean and the Scottish Highlands each years in their thousands. And his highly coloured (and highly priced and popular) Mediterranean and Highland scenes are representative of much of that decline of the English Watercolour already mentioned.

Hardie quotes Ruskin's Academy Notes of 1857 on T. M. Richardson, Junior—

> '... he seems always to conceive a Highland Landscape only as a rich medley of the same materials—a rocky bank, blue at one place and brown at another; some contorted Scottish firs; some ferns, some dogs, and some sportsmen; the whole contemplated under the cheery influence of champagne, and considered every way delightful.'

Richardson Junior somehow contrived by his colouring to make

[1] *Water-Colour Painting in Britain* by Martin Hardie: Vol. II, Batsford 1967, at page 230.

his Scottish Highlands look extraordinarily like the Mediterranean[2] but in spite of that his work brought (and still does bring) far higher prices than the work of his father, and I would think the son earned in five good years more than his father earned by painting in his whole life.

It is especially unfortunate that T.M. Senior should be thus dealt with after his death because he had very little good fortune during his life: and although many factors contributed to this it was due in some appreciable degree to his refusal to lower his sights and paint the pretty pictures which were to be seen everywhere when he died, and to his determination to continue to paint in the tradition of the eighteenth century in rather sombre colours and with complete integrity. But this obstacle to what some might think success, and others artistic damnation, was at least the result of his own choice. His other difficulties were not.

The first obstacle that fate put in his way was that although his father, George Richardson, was descended from a family of small landed proprietors in the Wark area of Northumberland, his father had been compelled to take the post of Headmaster of Sir Walter Blackett's St Andrew's Parish School, Newcastle, at a salary of £30 a year because he had been disinherited for marrying against his parents' will. The young Richardson was therefore brought up in the genteel poverty then thought suitable for the family of a Headmaster of a Charity School. His second difficulty was constant ill-health and threatened tuberculosis. His third difficulty was that although the works he exhibited won much critical acclaim so that he became the acknowledged leader of the very strong group of artists working in the 1820s and 1830s in Newcastle, prices obtainable for works of art in the North were low compared with prices nearer London, and whilst many gave praise to his pictures not so many actually bought them. As was stated in the introduction to the 1880 Edition of 'Memorials of Old Newcastle upon Tyne from Original Drawings by T. M. Richardson Senior'—

[2] Thomas Dibdin wrote with prophetic foreboding at page 398 of his *A Bibliographical Antiquarian and Picturesque Tour in the Northern Counties of England* (1838)—'Whilst I am writing these pages, the younger Mr Richardson is abroad, in Italy. All I anxiously hope, beg and entreat is that he will not *Italianize* Northumberland scenery.'

'During his lifetime he was certainly not appreciated; many of his best works hung for years on the walls of exhibitions and other places, unsold, and were parted with for ridiculously unremunerative prices. As an instance of this, the noble picture of "Newcastle from Gateshead Fell" was sold to the Corporation for fifty pounds.'

His fourth difficulty that was to endanger his own reputation—as the previous extract from Martin Hardie shows—is that in giving one of his sons the same names as his own he unwittingly created an element of confusion for some, as to which works were his own and which were his son's. For although the father more usually signed his work with his initials 'TMR' and the son more usually signed his work 'T. M. Richardson', this by no means always applies, and sometimes works by both are without any signature at all, and sometimes the father uses the longer signature. But at least one distinction between father and son can be clearly drawn. Whilst some of T.M. Senior's most distinguished work was done in oil and he must have painted almost as many oil paintings as watercolours I have never seen an oil painting by T.M. Junior and any work in oil by him must constitute the greatest rarity.

T. M. Richardson, as did his younger brother Moses Aaron Richardson (future printer, publisher, author, bookseller and finally, emigrant to Australia) went to the same Charity School of St Andrew's at which their father was Headmaster. The father proved an admirable headmaster and seems to have been happy enough away from his farmland at Wark; passionately fond of music, making his own instruments such as double bass, piano and organ, he was a great lover of landscape and nature, and T. M. Richardson inherited all his father's tastes. Richard Grainger, who was later to build the new Grainger Street and Grey Street, was a pupil at the same school but was slightly younger than Thomas and therefore was more a contemporary of his younger brother Moses.

Because of Thomas's precocious talent for drawing, he was at the age of fourteen apprenticed to the Newcastle engraver, Abraham Hunter, but soon Hunter was arrested for debt and died shortly after, so that the boy, rejecting his father's urging that he now study to be a surgeon, became apprenticed for seven years to John Gibson and Lancelot Usher, cabinet makers in Newcastle. By the terms of his indentures he was to receive no pay for the first four years of his servitude, four shillings per week for the fifth year, five shillings for the sixth and six shillings per week for the last year. By a curious coincidence the other apprentice in the firm, two years Richardson's senior, was Thomas Grainger, elder brother of Richard Grainger.

The sufferings of T. M. Richardson during his apprenticeship are well known. They were primarily due to the fact that the humane Usher dissolved his partnership with Gibson, and Gibson was a drunken, cruel and quarrelsome man on the downward path. So bad was his treatment of them that the two apprentices went before the magistrates and exercised their right to ask that the indentures be cancelled and they be set at liberty on the grounds of Gibson's misconduct. Gibson did not appear at the hearing and the Magistrates promised (or appeared to the two apprentices to be promising) that when Gibson appeared before him at the adjourned hearing they would be released. However at the final hearing the Magistrate rejected their application and they were both given the option of either serving their time to the end or being sent to the 'House of Correction'. Reluctantly they went back to Gibson, and Gibson made them work in the garret of his home where, the roof not being weatherproof, they were 'burnt up in summer and frozen in winter'. They were kept at work late, so that Richardson could find little time to practise his drawing and for a long period during the winter he had to walk to Lemington in the dark every morning on behalf of Gibson to make packing cases at the Prussian blue factory, and after the day's work had to walk the five miles back home and prepare for next morning. For this work at this time he was paid five shillings a week. It is generally thought that it was the privations suffered during his apprenticeship (of which only a few here have been mentioned) that destroyed his health and made his life a constant struggle against consumption and general illness.

As soon as he was out of his apprenticeship in 1801 T.M. married. He was then just over twenty-one years old and he was to continue in the cabinet making business for another five years after his marriage. He worked successfully as a cabinet maker but loathed the work and spent as much time in drawing as he could—not only drawing furniture for his trade but drawing outdoor subjects nearer to his heart. In 1806 the sudden death of his father gave him the opportunity to be freed from a life he detested when he was offered the opportunity to succeed his father as Headmaster—at the same salary of £30 a year! He accepted and showed aptitude for the work like his father but, in 1813 his health broke down, he began to spit blood and became very feeble and a sea voyage and a change of air was recommended. That is how at the age of twenty-eight years, on his first visit to London, he found himself looking at David Cox's watercolour of Conway Castle in a picture dealer's window in the Strand—an experience which Richardson always maintained changed the whole course of his life.

Richardson at the time of this visit had never seen any exhibition of pictures, and had never even previously heard of David Cox. He attempted to buy the watercolour, but the price of ten guineas was not only far too much for him to pay (over a third of one year's salary) but opened his eyes also to what could be earned by painting pictures. He often told the story of how he looked at the picture for over an hour through the window, absorbing the lessons it held for him and his future, and he determined to return to Newcastle and prove that he could and would do as well. Cox's picture of Conway Castle exercised such an influence over his life as an example of artistic perfection that he often said he wished he could buy the drawing and would pay almost any price for it if he could find it. Certainly after his return to Newcastle, in addition to his normal school work, he painted and drew more than ever before with new hope, and his pupils and their parents, and others, seeing and admiring his pictures and watercolours, came in increasing numbers to him to learn drawing and painting until there was no doubt in his own mind that in art and in art teaching there lay his true vocation. As his pupils for drawing and painting increased, and as his own work became more accomplished—he was to an amazing extent entirely self-taught—there came the choice as to whether he dare resign his Headmastership which was becoming increasingly another work of drudgery and which interfered with the practice of his art, but which at least gave him a home and some semblance of security at £30 a year. It is the difficult choice which many artists have had to make in every generation, and the choice was made even more difficult by the fact that George his eldest son had been born in 1808 and Edward in 1810.

It was not until 1813 (the very year that T. M. Richardson, Junior was born) that he felt he had made sufficient progress and gained sufficient confidence to resign his Headmastership and so come to rely on his art alone to keep himself and his family. Respected and admired as he was to become as the leader and promoter of artistic activity and taste in the town, it is doubtful whether he was henceforth ever free for long from financial anxiety, although there is no doubt he gained great satisfaction from his roles as painter, teacher and promoter of exhibitions, and no one loved the company of his fellow artists more, or was happier in their company.

Within a year after he had resigned his Headmastership his first oil painting 'VIEW OF THE OLD FISHMARKET, Newcastle upon Tyne' was hung in the Royal Academy and attracted much favourable attention and he continued to exhibit many pictures there until 1845. After resigning his Headmastership he had taken up residence with his wife and family in a house in Brunswick Place, Newcastle, on the present site of which there was until the last year or so a plaque commemorating the fact; and on 23rd September, 1822, with the assistance of Thomas and Robert Bewick, Henry Perlee Parker, the painter, and John Dobson, he inaugurated at his own Brunswick Place home the first Fine Art Exhibition in the North of England to which he himself contributed fourteen pictures.

This was the first exhibition to be held by the 'Northumberland Institution FOR THE PROMOTION OF THE FINE ARTS', an Institution formed for professional and amateur artists solely on the initiative of Richardson in 1822, and it is interesting to discover that its President was the gifted amateur watercolourist Edward Swinburne of Capheaton Hall, Richardson himself was Treasurer, and on the Committee sat Thomas Bewick and his son Robert,

Joseph Crawhall (the grandfather of the Joseph Crawhall who was to make his name as an animal painter), John Dobson, Henry Perlee Parker (1795-1873) a notable painter of public events and local personalities and James Ramsay an extremely competent local portrait painter. Richardson was to hold exhibitions of paintings and watercolours at his home, sometimes as many as three or four exhibitions in a year, until 1828, and whilst these exhibitions attracted critical acclaim and grew in reputation throughout the six years they were held in Richardson's home, the number of pictures bought continued to be disappointing, since picture buying (like most other things) is a habit in which fashion plays a part, and until the advent of T. M. Richardson, the middle classes in Newcastle had never been given any opportunity or invitation to form the habit.

At this first exhibition in 1822 there were 162 paintings and watercolours. The entrance fee was one shilling (which seems expensive for those days), catalogues were 6d. and you could buy a season ticket for five shillings. The vast majority of the exhibits were by local artists or by artists with local connections, but this would not detract from the high standard because this truly was Newcastle's Golden Age for artistic achievement. Stretching back over the previous forty years there had been the Beilby's painting on glass, Bewick's woodcuts, silversmiths like Langlands, John Robertson, Isaac Cookson and Robert Watson who had carried on the earlier work of the seventeenth-century William Ramsay to a level of artistry at which the Newcastle silversmiths had no superior in any city in England. It was the same with eighteenth-century architects like William Newton and David Stephenson and William Stokoe and now there were the younger men like Thomas Oliver and the Greens, and Dobson and Wardle and Walker just coming along.

The local painters matched up to this level of general excellence —men like George Balmer, Luke Clennell, J. W. Carmichael in addition to those already mentioned—and there were those, born in Newcastle although now practising art elsewhere, who still regarded Newcastle as their home town and sent exhibits—men like James Ewbank, a wonderful painter at his best, whose swift rise to wealth and success in Edinburgh was succeeded by an equally sudden descent to misery, William Nicholson who became a founder member of the Royal Scottish Academy, and others. But at this first exhibition in September 1822 there was also shown in addition to these, an animal painting by the great James Ward, an oil painting 'Macbeth and THE WITCHES' by John Martin which must be the painting that is now in the possession of the Scottish National Gallery in Edinburgh, and work by Copley Fielding.

From 1822 to 1828 Richardson worked with great industry showing up to twenty paintings and watercolours at the Exhibitions and painting and selling as many as he could in between exhibitions to support his growing family. But there were some, especially some members of the Corporation, who thought that they and the City could surpass what Richardson was achieving merely in his own house. So Richard Grainger in 1827 began the building (to Dobson's design) of the classical stone building at 41 Blackett Street which it was felt would be more in keeping with the City's growing sense of importance, and which was opened on 11th June, 1828, as the Academy of Arts. Richardson, assisted by H. P. Parker, was still to organize for several years the exhibitions of the Institution held in the Academy—a building truly described in the *Newcastle Courant* of 21st June, 1828, as 'an honour and ornament to the Town'—but the exhibitions were to lose the more personal quality of Richardson's taste and discrimination, since the exhibitions in their new and more spacious home had to consist of more pictures (there were about 300 pictures exhibited at the first 1828 Academy Exhibition as compared with 162 at the first Brunswick Place Exhibition in 1822). When an exhibition becomes as large as this, a feeling grows that it has to be representative of what is then being painted —good or bad—rather than consisting of pictures (as formerly) which Richardson had liked and wanted to show in his own home.

At this first Exhibition in the new Academy of Art—'the best exhibition of pictures ever seen in Newcastle'—the *Newcastle Courant* called it, in addition to a multitude of paintings by most of the artists already mentioned as previously exhibiting in Brunswick Place, there were works by Francis Danby ARA, William Linton, a still life painting by the famous George Lance, works by William Mulready RA, A. W. Calcott RA, a Portrait of Sir

Matthew White Ridley by John Jackson RA (friend of Haydon and Wilkie), work by the Berwick painter Thomas Sword Good and two watercolours by J. M. W. Turner which incurred the wrath of the *Newcastle Courant* critic—'The drawings certainly give the spectator no very exalted idea of the great painter. Indeed without his name they would not be noticed at all. The execution is laboured and not effective. In short, they are indifferent pictures from an old hand.'

There was undoubtedly a feeling, which was to grow stronger with successive exhibitions in the Academy, that whilst the local artists and those with local connections were showing their best work, the London artists were sending only their indifferent. And even at the very first 1828 Exhibition the *Courant* critic felt it necessary on 14th July, 1828, to issue this warning to London painters—'It is a mistaken notion to imagine that bad pictures will sell more readily in county towns. With connoisseurs taste is everywhere much the same ... we are not so deficient in discernment here as to mistake bad pictures for good, or to purchase bad when good are to be had at other markets.'

Richardson continued to organize the exhibitions at the Blackett Street Academy for several years, but although artistically they won praise not as many pictures were sold as Richardson had a right to expect and few exhibitions could be regarded as commercially successful, although many fine and interesting exhibitions were organized by him. But without his initiative in 1822, no exhibitions would have been held in Newcastle, the Academy would never have been built, and without the atmosphere of artistic enterprise which his leadership in the town produced, the great architectural plans of Grainger for the 1830s might not have won the Corporation's support and would have been still-born. For several years Richardson was to make the Academy the centre of Newcastle's artistic life, and a home and exhibition centre for its artists, and it seems pitiful that this potentially still gracious classical building (the unsightly shop front could be removed and the unity of the design restored) is to be demolished instead of an attempt being made to restore it to its former elegance and to make it a feature of any new development.

So far as T. M. Richardson's own work was concerned, his

pictures sold better as his fame increased until his name became well known in London, but his prices remained low in comparison with those obtainable by other painters of similar calibre elsewhere. For his very best work in oils he could expect at the most £70-£80 and for watercolours about £30—but his average would be less than half of these prices. He married a second time at some uncertain date and by his second wife also had three sons—Henry Burden, Charles, and John Isaac who was only eleven years old when his father died. So that he always had too many claims on his earnings and never had any to spare. As he wrote to a friend[3] 'Although I have not realized anything by my profession, I have been enabled to bring up a very large family respectably; I have had a large share of sickness and death and although I cannot say of myself as the late Benjamin West said of artists in general, that they are "companions of kings and emperors", yet can I truly affirm from being a poor joiner lad, by my own industry I have become the companion of the noble and the gentle, having visited at their residences and sat at their tables ... I must say however that one of the grand mistakes of my life has been my neglecting to take up my residence in London twenty or thirty years ago.'

In 1831 Richardson formed the Northern Society of Painters in Water Colours and in the same year he organized the first exhibition at the Academy confined to watercolours alone, all the previous exhibitions having been mixed. After a few years the Academy exhibitions ceased to be organized by Richardson and whether the primary reason for this was simply the time and cost to Richardson of organizing exhibitions which were not commercially successful or whether it was due primarily, in the cryptic words of the *Newcastle Courant*[4] to

'the interference of some individuals who considered that such an institution should not be in the hands of a private person but be the property and business of many ... and consequently exhibitions ceased to exist in our town.'

Characteristically, in the Autumn of 1847—only a few months before he died—he reverted to his old idea of an exhibition in

---
[3] *Newcastle Courant*, 18th March, 1848.
[4] *Newcastle Courant*, 18th March, 1848.

his own home (by this date in Blackett Street) consisting of works which he would like to exhibit under his own roof consisting mainly, but not wholly, of his own works with some of his family's. This exhibition was highly praised by press and critics, but commercially was a failure and as the *Newcastle Courant* wrote 'Caused its projector considerable pecuniary loss and materially embittered his few remaining days'. But he was still up to the date of his last illness engaged in preparing drawings and plates as illustrations for the new History of Newcastle upon Tyne by his brother Moses Aaron: but this was never published and the ill fortune that seemed to dog him had already resulted in previous projects with his younger brother coming to nothing, such as the project in 1833 to publish by subscription 'Castles of the English and Scottish Borders', excessive delays between the appearances of the parts causing the whole scheme to collapse after only two numbers had been published.

He died on 7th March, 1848, after a painful illness lasting seven weeks. A contemporary describes how towards the end he had a horror of going to bed, refused to go, and spent days crouching in his chair until seven days before he died he was carried to his bed. The mourners who followed his coffin to the grave in the family burial place in Jesmond Cemetery included, apart from his family, Richard Grainger, the Reverend John Collingwood Bruce, John Dobson, Benjamin Green the architect of Newcastle's magnificent Theatre Royal, William Bell Scott and many artists whom he had advised and helped during his life.

There was a long obituary notice of him published in the *Newcastle Courant*. It gives a vivid word picture of the painter by one who knew him—

'He was a short, thick-set man, and his face exhibited marks of years of acute suffering. Otherwise, there was an expression of kindliness on his features which experience certainly did not belie, and though no stranger to polite society and the amenities of life, he was destitute of the art of flattery, or even of so much of design as to induce him to comport himself differently before a nobleman than he did in the presence of his intimate friends. He retained too the sonorous and expres-

ELDON SQUARE (now partially demolished)

JOHN DOBSON, 1787-1865

(by courtesy of Mr and Mrs I. S. Duncan)
PRESTWICK LODGE

NUNNYKIRK, FRONT ENTRANCE (*Country Life*)

NUNNYKIRK, GARDEN FRONT

(*Country Life*)

(Country Life)

THE HALL AT NUNNYKIRK

THE HALL AT LONGHIRST

(*Country Life*)

MELDON PARK, GARDEN FRONT

(*Country Life*)

(Country Life)

MELDON PARK, MAIN ENTRANCE

MONKWEARMOUTH RAILWAY STATION (Sunderland Corporation)

(Scottish National Portrait Gallery)
SELF-PORTRAIT, WILLIAM BELL SCOTT

(National Gallery of Scotland)
WILLIAM BELL SCOTT
Oil painting by David Scott

(by courtesy of the National Trust, Wallington)
PAULINE, LADY TREVELYAN
Oil painting by William Bell Scott

(by kind permission of the Trevelyan family)
W. B. SCOTT (*left*), D. G. ROSSETTI, JOHN RUSKIN

STILL LIFE by William Bell Scott (Laing Art Gallery)

JACK COMMON

sive dialect of the north and took no pains to conceal his native peculiarities; he knew better how to gain the esteem of his contemporaries, than by attempting to clip his language or assume any species of affectation.'

It could accurately be said—and an obituary notice did say it—that for a period close upon thirty years the career of this man was the history of pictorial art in Newcastle upon Tyne— and at a period of its greatest achievement. Without him, it would never have happened at all, and the most important aspect of his work was that he was the first artist to try in Newcastle to make a painter's life and work a matter of concern to the citizens of his own town, the first to attempt by exhibitions, by writing, by teaching, by painting, to break down the barrier between the artist and the indifferent majority. It is a difficult task, and failure and loss is still the fate of those who make the attempt in most places today.

Even to the very end of his days his colours were subdued yet rich—as great a contrast as can be imagined with the colours used by his sons, all of whom were talented watercolour painters without the taste and strength to escape from the fashion and spirit of their period. He never painted abroad so never felt tempted to use the high colours and the cobalt which became almost obligatory for such scenes. All his works were set in Northumberland, or on the Scottish side of the Border, or in Cumberland, Westmorland, Yorkshire, North Wales, Greenwich and the Thames—the latter done on holidays in search of better health.

He should not be judged by the tired examples of his work which not infrequently find their way into the salerooms. An artist is to be judged by the best of his work which constitutes in most cases only a relatively small proportion of his painting, and the best examples of Richardson's work have been hung in the drawing rooms of the same families for generations and rarely are to be seen in public. But if he is judged by the best examples of his work which are to be seen in the Newcastle Laing Art Gallery, and the examples illustrated here, and the best which I have seen in other collections, public and private, then he is entitled to a very high place indeed, his landscapes comparing with the very best of the English School and his sunset skies and seas reminding one of Turner at his best, and making nonsense of Martin Hardie's curt dismissal. As with most painters, there is a great gulf between his best work and his mediocre, and it is certain—like most painters who have large families to support—that he painted too many pictures; William Etty (to take one particular case amongst many) painted many indifferent paintings, and if these are the only ones that the critic sees he will have a completely false view of Etty's stature as a painter; but once he has seen the Etty landscapes, predating Impressionism by thirty years or more, and the portraits and the still life paintings in the gallery of his birthplace at York, Etty moves at once into a totally different class from where his mediocre work would seem to put him. Similarly, the best work of Thomas Miles Richardson senior, and there is a lot of it, places him very close to the first rank of the English School of painters and watercolourists.

CHAPTER FIVE

Richard Grainger

'He had had great pleasure in giving them (his streets) up to the town ... he had a taste for art, and was not bound to decorate his houses in the manner the Commissioners had seen, but did it because it pleased him to do it, although the cost had probably been not less than £100,000.'
Richard Grainger's evidence to the Cholera Commissioners in 1854.

THERE are no more derisive words in the planning dictionary than 'piece-meal and patchwork development'. Yet this is precisely what has created the element of surprise in our towns and villages, has ensured intriguing differences in roof levels and style, has produced variegated streets leading into planned squares and crescents, each period and each method making its contribution to a variegated pattern held together by the unifying colours of building materials made out of the nearby quarry or clay.

It is precisely 'comprehensive re-development'—the most authoritative text in the modern bureaucratic bible—that has produced the drab monotony of the staining and streaking concrete of the 'shopping precincts', the 'prestige blocks' which should confer only odium, the housing estates where every interesting slope and fold in the ground has been bulldozed out; and—most important of all—which has licensed the destruction of every building that lies in its path because those responsible lack the imagination to fit into a design any interesting old buildings already there. It is so much easier to clear the whole area and start with the desert that is called, 'a clean site'.

This is a national problem, and probably an international one too. The centres of old towns everywhere are endangered—and in many places have been destroyed—by the simple fact that the site is much more valuable than the old building on it (however great its architectural merit), and the rateable value and rents derived from a ten storey 'office block and shopping precinct' is so much greater, that all over Britain an apparently irresistible combination of private and municipal money making has done irretrievable damage already. This has led to the tower block wreckage we see today in so many of our cities.

It is sometimes said that the catastrophic results of 'comprehensive re-development' are because planners and architects—unlike the landowning and private planners of the eighteenth and early nineteenth centuries on whose rapidly diminishing capital of landscape beauty this country is now living—have not sufficient time to think out their problems, have to plan on a vastly greater scale than before, and have not had the leisure, the education and the means to develop an eye and taste of their own.

Yet there was one early nineteenth-century builder and town planner born in crushing poverty, who had little leisure and even less education in the Arts, leaving his Charity School at the age of twelve, who built at breathless speed with other people's money on a scale as great or greater than most of today's City Planning; and yet who built streets and buildings in stone of such elegance and beauty to make Newcastle at the end of his day, in Professor Pevsner's words 'the best designed Victorian town in England and indeed the best designed large city in England altogether'.[1]

In retrospect his achievement is even more remarkable—for he designed the first planned *commercial centre* of a City in this country—and turned it into a thing of delight. There had been other planners before him, Wood building his graceful crescents in Bath, Adam his squares in Edinburgh, Carr his houses in York—but they built on the periphery of their Cities and for living only; Grainger was the first town planner, and he built the graceful curving Grey Street and the wide and beautiful

---

[1] N. Pevsner, *The Buildings of Northumberland*, 1957, p. 56 (Penguin Books).

Grainger Street and the streets leading off and into them for working and living in, the beautiful pilastered and stone carved buildings having shops, big and small at street level, and houses above the shops for their owners and their servants to live and sleep in. The only possible analogy is the original Nash design for Regent Street in London and that was in stucco as compared with the more honest stone of Grainger's new City. Grainger evolved a style of building that combined commercial convenience with a civic and architectural dignity beyond anything achieved by any builder before or since.

It is Grainger's achievement of course which still—in spite of the amount of banal and out of scale building that has been allowed to take place—makes the very air and atmosphere in Newcastle's centre feel so different from other commercial cities such as Birmingham or Manchester. Even to the unseeing eye of someone who does not look above the shop windows to pediment, frieze, and pilaster to the overall street design, no one in the Grey Street, Grainger Street or the former Eldon Square area (now partially demolished) could doubt that he was in a city centre with a distinctive atmosphere worthy of a regional capital —and not in a mere straggle of streets and shops leading pointlessly on to more streets and shops as is the impression in most other large cities. Whether this atmosphere can survive the modern growth and elephantiasis that threatens to dwarf Grainger's achievement is a matter for grave doubt.

Richard Grainger, second son of Thomas Grainger 'a porter pokeman gannin' on the quay' was born in an upstairs tenement of two rooms in High Friar Lane, Newcastle, on 9th October, 1797. He went to St Andrew's Parish Charity School where T. M. Richardson's father was Headmaster and, his father dying early, Grainger whilst at school, was supported entirely by a resourceful mother's skill at sewing and glove making. In 1809 he was bound to John Brown carpenter, and his elder brother George having served indentures as a bricklayer, the two of them in about 1816 began business as jobbing builders in the smallest possible way. His brother George died shortly after the commencement of their partnership—in 1817 or 1818—so that Richard was left to carry on alone. It was towards the end of 1818 that Grainger met the man who was to set him on the path to success—the rich (although later bankrupt) Methodist, Alderman William Batson who lived at Higham Dykes, a beautiful Queen Anne brick house between Ponteland and Belsay still happily standing and well cared for.

Alderman Batson, obviously impressed by the young Grainger's personality and workmanship, contracted him to build in 1819 a new street, of particularly delightful small Georgian houses which Batson called Higham Place. Harriet Martineau records[2] that so anxious was Grainger to succeed in this first important contract that he worked from 3.00 a.m. to 9.00 p.m. each day. Little present regard has been shown for Grainger's first street, and within the last few years, without any public protest, the whole street has been demolished save for three houses now overshadowed by a building totally out of scale with them.

With the money obtained from this contract Grainger was now able to work on a bigger scale, building houses in New Bridge Street and Carliol Street and within a year or so, was able to marry Rachel Arundale the daughter of a prosperous Newcastle tanner who was to bear him thirteen children—all of whose names are commemorated in the street names of the Elswick area, an area that was to bring Grainger near to financial disaster. But the dowry from this marriage enabled him in 1824 to build thirty-one brick houses in Blackett Street, still to be seen today (but soon to be demolished) extending from the Eldon Square area to Percy Street. This street was designed by Thomas Oliver, and in 1825 Grainger began to build Eldon Square to Dobson's designs—although the Square was not completed with the impressive central section of the Northern Counties' Club until about 1832.

Pevsner[3] treats the building of Eldon Square as one of the turning points in Newcastle's architectural history (as its demolition must also be treated)

'... here indeed a claim to formality and monumentality was staked that was new to the town and must at once have

[2] In the Penny Magazine of The Society for the Diffusion of Useful Knowledge (No. 515, 11th April, 1840).
[3] *Buildings of England*: Northumberland, 1957, p. 252.

doomed the modest houses of Saville Row ... At that time nothing yet existed of Grainger Street and Grey Street, that is the centre of Newcastle except for Mosley Street was still narrow and unplanned. The spaciousness of Eldon Square was a thing quite unheard-of. So was the size of the ranges surrounding the Square, and so was also their uniform design.'

However, (although Newcastle did not then know it) this was only the beginning.

In 1827 Grainger built St Mary's Place to Dobson's reticent and tasteful design, adjacent to the Church of St Thomas The Martyr at Barras Bridge which Dobson had just completed, and very slightly Gothicized to harmonize with it. In 1829 he began an even more massive enterprise than Eldon Square when he began the building of Leazes Terrace, Leazes Crescent and Leazes Place to designs by Thomas Oliver, and in June 1831 began to build the Royal Arcade to designs by either Dobson or Oliver—another tremendous undertaking of which the *Newcastle Journal* of 19th May, 1832, said 'This magnificent building ... cannot fail to become a prominent ornament to the town and an object of attraction to every intelligent visitor ... Some idea may be formed of the great skill, assiduity and judgement by which the various operations have been directed by Mr Grainger when we state that although all the apartments, offices, shops and public rooms are expected to be fully occupied in the course of a few weeks, it is not yet twelve months since the first stone was laid.'

And so on 30th July, 1833, a great public dinner was held in Newcastle, the Mayor John Brandling presiding, and several M.P.s attending, at which Grainger was presented with a silver tureen and salver to mark the town's appreciation of what he had achieved. He was only thirty-six years of age, his mother who had kept him by her sewing was still alive, the values of the main buildings he had erected were calculated in 1833 to be —early buildings £45,000, Eldon Square £30,000, Leazes Area, £80,000, Royal Arcade £40,000—and he had not yet even begun his main work!

Newcastle began on the steep northern bank of the River

Tyne and whilst the steepness made Newcastle one of the most melodramatically sited of towns, the ravines running down bearing the swiftly running Skinner, Lort, and Pandon Burns into the Tyne, made communications difficult. On these steep banks grew the medieval and Elizabethan town with the crowded chares that ran up and down and across them, a few of the Elizabethan timber houses still surviving today on the Quayside. Although the Castle area was to the north and on top of the River Bank, Newcastle's attempt to develop northwards proceeded only slowly, the core of the town still remaining close to the River and Castle Keep even at the end of the seventeenth century. It is for example significant that when in 1656 Trollap was asked to design a new Newcastle Exchange, he built it on the site of the old one at the water's edge, rather than on the high ground to the north, and Mansion House Wharf reminds us that the Mansion House was indeed built there in 1691 at the foot of Tuthill Stairs. So steep were the Tyne's banks that even in the seventeenth century progress up and down was by means of stairs such as Croft Stairs, King Stairs, the Long Stairs, and Dog Leap Stairs.

With the growing commercial prosperity of the eighteenth century there began the overflow into the rural and more pleasant areas of the upper town, and the roads leading to and from the walls of the City became lined with merchants' houses; Alderman Mosley sponsored between 1784 and 1789 the filling in of that open sewer, the Lort Burn, to become Dean Street, Mosley Street was built with David Stevenson's Theatre Royal sited there, William Newton expressed the town's growing feeling for expansive elegance when in 1776 he built the Assembly Rooms, and Stephenson built the classical round Church of All Saints between 1786 and 1789. These efforts between 1766 and 1789 with the building of Georgian Squares and streets like Charlotte Square and Clavering Place, marked the emergence of Newcastle as a Georgian town just a few years before Grainger's birth.

Yet it must not be thought, even before the rebuilding achieved by Alderman Mosley and David Stephenson in the 1780s, that Newcastle had been an ordinary town. William Camden in 1609 described Newcastle as 'the glory of all the towns in this country', and in 1633 Sir William Brereton of Cheshire wrote—'Newcastle is beyond all compare the fairest and richest town in England, inferior for wealth and building to no city save London and Bristol'. John Wesley said that were he not 'journeying to Heaven' he could not wish for a more pleasant abiding place than Newcastle. Even before the Grainger transformation, no provincial town could provide the approaching visitor with a more dramatic cluster of buildings than Stokoe's Greek Temple of a Moothall at the side of the Norman Castle Keep, with the Lantern Tower of St Nicholas in the background; and below them on the Quayside was Trollap's Guildhall, the river with its bridges, and to the right, David Stephenson's round classical church.

But in Grainger's time standing in the way of further development to the north were the many acres of Sir Walter Blackett's great house and gardens in what is now the Market Street and Blackett Street area, and also the open spaces of the Nun's Field area now occupied by Nun Street, the vegetable market, and part of Grainger Street. Sir Walter's house was described by Henry Bourne in his *History of Newcastle* (1736) as the most stately and magnificent 'of any house in the whole kingdom within a walled town'. In 1782 George Anderson, a wealthy builder, acquired the property which became known as Anderson Place, and the formal gardens stretching along Northumberland Street with other extensive gardens in the town including Carliol Croft, stood in the way of further development. Harriet Martineau states[4] that Grainger was early impressed with 'the uselessness of Anderson Place and the availability of extensive stone quarries nearby'. It is obvious from the foregoing that, for an energetic and ambitious builder like Grainger, Newcastle as they now would say, was 'ripe for development' and it will be made plain that Grainger worked with ruthless determination either to demolish existing buildings and to rebuild, or to build on pleasant open spaces and gardens. One has little doubt that had there been in existence any Newcastle Amenity Society or any Society for the Protection of Ancient Buildings there would have been vehement protests; and they would, within the year, have been proved wrong in so protesting by the sight of the startling beauty of the buildings that Grainger put in their place.

[4] *The Penny Magazine*, No. 515, 11th April, 1840.

I do not know of any case in modern times where such justification could have been put forward for any 'development', and the one thing that any Amenity Society can be sure of today is that almost any threatened building, whatever its architectural quality, will be replaced by a worse one.

Grainger was fortunate in that although David Stephenson, William Newton and William Stokoe were now either dead or retired, a group of architects with a love and understanding of the classical style in building had grown up to take their place. Thomas Oliver, John Dobson, John Green and his son Benjamin, constituted the strongest team of architects ever to be working at one time in Newcastle—and Grainger used them all; but he also created a strong team of his own office architects including two men, Wardle and Walker, who as we shall see, were of more than ordinary talent; and Grainger himself knew exactly the effects he wanted to achieve and the sort of design he wanted and although wise enough to employ the rich architectural talent at his disposal must have played a considerable part in the planning of the design—as is indicated by the words he spoke to the Cholera Commissioners in 1854.

Although Grainger was a builder with a keen interest in design, only the two architects, Dobson and Oliver, had put forward proposals to the Common Council before 1832 (i.e., by the time the Royal Arcade was completed) for the total replanning of Central Newcastle. The money resources required were so vast, and the complexities involved in overcoming the private ownerships and vested interests so great, that both schemes were still-born. But the Town Clerk, John Clayton, much impressed with Grainger's personality, obviously made up his mind that Grainger was the man with the determination and organizing ability to rebuild the town centre. This Clayton was the son of the former Town Clerk, Nathaniel Clayton, who had presided over some of the late eighteenth-century improvements of Alderman Mosley and David Stephenson. Nathaniel Clayton had held office as Town Clerk from 1785 to 1822 when John succeeded him holding office until 1867. He lived on at his home at Chesters near the Roman Wall pursuing his antiquarian interests until he died at the age of ninety-eight in 1890.

Clayton was far-seeing, wise, immensely respected, and—

because in those days a solicitor who was a Town Clerk could also continue in private practice and hold other lucrative appointments—extremely rich. An anonymous councillor gives an interesting word picture of him—[5]

'Has all the craft and subtlety of the devil. Great talents, indefatigable industry, immense wealth and wonderful tact and facility in conducting business, give him an influence in society rarely possessed by one individual ... can do things with impunity that would damn an ordinary man. A good voice, speaks well and never wastes a word. Has a careworn but shy countenance, and spare person ...'

This was the man who early in 1834, the year after that public dinner which marked the beginning of a new stage in Grainger's progress, was to become until Grainger's death, his personal solicitor, his private adviser, his saviour from bankruptcy, and who was to use all his great influence with the Common Council for the acceptance of Grainger's plans for the building of Grey Street and Grainger Street which was to mark the climax both of his own career and of the town's architectural development.

On 22nd May, 1834, Grainger's detailed proposals for a new Town Centre appeared in the Common Council Minute Books the minute ending—'Ordered that a special Common Council be called for 12th June at 11 a.m. in the Mayor's Chamber, and that a lithographed plan of Mr Grainger's proposals, with a printed statement of the case, be circulated to members and to the inhabitants of the town'. When the plans were exhibited in the Royal Arcade complete with elevational and sectional drawings (indicating that long and careful preparation in conjunction with his architects and Clayton, had preceded his approach to the Council) the public interest and enthusiasm was unprecedented. The *Newcastle Journal* said[6] '... from the magnitude of those undertakings which Mr Grainger has already successfully executed, the public mind had been prepared to expect that there

---
[5] The Corporation Annual or Recollections (not random) of the First Reformed Town Council of the Borough of Newcastle-upon-Tyne by a late councillor, 3rd Edition 1836, published by W. Boas.
[6] 31st May, 1834.

was something more than usually grand and extensive in the proposed change, but we will venture to affirm that of the thousands who have made themselves acquainted with Mr Grainger's plans, there is not one but has acknowledged that they previously had no conception of their practicality, extent and splendour'.

To summarize the main points of the plan, it undertook to continue Dean Street across Mosley Street to the North by a new street then called New Dean Street, later called Upper Dean Street and by the time it was completed (1837)—Grey Street; to continue a second new main street from the top of New Dean Street to the top of the Bigg Market (this was to be Grainger Street) and a third main street now known as Clayton Street and Clayton Street West; to build a new theatre in New Dean Street (the present Theatre Royal) in place of the Theatre Royal in Mosley Street which Grainger had to demolish to make New Dean Street: and from the main streets described there were to be branch streets—now Shakespeare Street, Hood Street, Nun Street, Nelson Street—all, enthused the *Newcastle Journal*[7] 'fronted with polished stone, chastely ornamented, the interior being filled up with every available requisite both as dwellings and places of business'.

The *Newcastle Journal* in its same issue disclosed that ground already purchased by Grainger with this scheme in mind had cost £25,000, paving and flagging of the new streets alone was estimated to cost £6,000 more with an additional £7,000 for the approaches, 'making a total of £38,000 without the laying of a single stone for the costly buildings'. The sheets in Mr Small's auction room in the Royal Arcade where the plans were exhibited, after only a few days carried 5,000 signatures in favour of the plans, with only 300 against; and when on Tuesday, 15th July, 1834, the Council, doubtless guided by the advice of their learned Town Clerk, formally approved the plan, the bells of St Nicholas Cathedral were rung to celebrate the event and there was 'general rejoicing throughout the town'.

Two things immediately stand out from even the above brief summary of the plan. First that Grainger must have come to agreement with George Anderson's executors (he had died in

[7] 31st May, 1834.

1831) to purchase Anderson Place (the agreed price was £50,000 as became clear later) and the adjoining Nun's Field; secondly, that the money involved in these schemes was so enormous that John Clayton must have opened up to Grainger a supply of money quite outside even Grainger's capacity to raise. For it must be remembered that the Corporation (save for the new Markets) were not going to buy anything from Grainger—the builder was to finance the building of them himself, enjoy the rents from them if he retained the freehold, and bear the whole risk if they were not let at rents profitable enough to make the whole gargantuan enterprise, including the roads and paving, profitable—or having built the shops and houses above them, he would either have to mortgage them or—as a last resort—dispose of the freeholds at a price which would show a profit to enable him to go forward with the remainder of the plan. Although the activities of property companies backed with vast resources from Insurance Companies and other institutions has familiarized the second half of the twentieth century with property development and speculation (usually with the most unhappy aesthetic results) this was property development and not speculation (for Grainger always hoped to retain the freeholds and lease what he had built on half yearly or quarterly tenancies) but on a scale and with financial risks unprecedented at this date. It must have looked a daunting prospect sometimes even to the ebullient and optimistic Grainger, but if he felt any doubts he never showed them in public.

The method which Grainger employed to finance his vast building schemes[8] was quite simply to build and then mortgage and with the mortgage money to build again and so on and so on. He always hoped to retain the freeholds, and thanks to John Clayton's guidance he did manage to retain most of them, even throughout his darkest days—but it was his descendents, benefiting from the enormous rise in property values and rents following his death, who were to reap the harvest of his enterprise and imagination. Because of what seems at times, to be an almost obsessive desire to continue to build—instead of pausing and reaping the fruit of what he had already built—at no time in

[8] The matter is gone into in detail in pages 103-121 in *Tyneside Classical* by Lyall Wilkes and Gordon Dodds (John Murray, 1964).

his career had he ever much money of his own; doubtless he could comfort himself with the thought that although he might not have much (or any) money in the bank, he was potentially an immensely rich man since he was the freehold owner of magnificent properties; but as soon as he could raise sufficient money from them by way of mortgage to enable him to begin a new building, a new street, a new scheme, the money would go into that, leaving Grainger continuously at the mercy of his mortgagees.

Where Grainger got £50,000 to buy Anderson Place we do not know; if Grainger had such a sum, or indeed any substantial sum at all of his own freely available for the purchase, then he was never to be in such a happy position again—once again the likelihood is by way of mortgage and loan, bearing in mind that £38,000 was needed plus £50,000 for the purchase of Anderson Place before a single rentable or mortgageable asset could be built. But what can be said with certainty is that John Clayton had already lent Grainger substantial sums of money of his own before 1834, had introduced him to the Backhouse family, the owners of the Northumberland and Durham District Banking Company, and that the list of names of those who were his Mortgagees is a list of the leading citizens of the town, its leading Methodists, Quaker Bankers, and Lawyers especially. On this perilous engine of credit Grainger steered his course without disaster until 1839 and produced the best architecture that Newcastle has ever known.

What impressed the general public was not only the magnificent buildings he built, but the speed with which he built them. The Common Council had approved the plans on 15th July, 1834, and at once Grainger began to clear the ground on the Nun's Field for the laying out of the new Vegetable and Butcher Markets, hundreds of horses and carts being used to take the soil from the Nun's Field to fill in the Upper Lort Burn ravine to prepare for the building of what is now Grey Street: he had bricks made on the spot as he had done when building Eldon Square. On 24th May, 1836, Grainger signed the contract with the owners of the old Theatre Royal in Mosley Street to build them the new and beautiful Theatre Royal in the proposed new Upper Dean Street (architect Benjamin Green) and three hours after the contract was signed the chimneys were down and within a day or so the old theatre had disappeared.[9] Grainger's contract with the Corporation to build them a new Flesh and Vegetable Market for £36,290 (Grainger giving them £15,000 for their old Flesh Market which had only been built in 1808) was only signed on 25th December, 1834, but by 24th October, 1835, the famous celebration dinner was held in the Vegetable Market to celebrate the completion of the 180 Butchers' Shops and the many other shops and streets of the Market.

This famous dinner is the subject of the painting by Henry Purlee Parker now in the Laing Art Gallery, and gives a good impression of the vast scale of these new markets—only Hungerford Market and Covent Garden in London and St John's of Liverpool excelling them in size; but for architectural grace these stone markets with their fountains and elaborate gas lamps were declared by the *Newcastle Journal* to be 'the most magnificent in the world'. By 5th October, 1835, the new streets were able to be named by the Common Council and Grainger's work would, it was clear, succeed at last in moving the centre of the Town away from the quay and Castle Keep area. By 7th June, 1837, the new streets were completed, and flagged, the hundreds of shops and houses occupied, and in 1838 Benjamin Green's column to Earl Grey provided the dramatic new centrifugal point to the whole city.

Although Grainger Street and Grey Street were his most elaborately designed streets and have won Grainger and Newcastle great acclaim—Gladstone writing[10] 'Grey Street—I think our best modern street' and Professor Pevsner claiming it[11] as 'one of the best streets in England'—the great domes of the Central Arcade and Exchange and the fine stone work in the other streets such as Clayton Street and Hood Street, Nun Street

[9] Thomas Dibdin wrote in his *A Bibliographical Antiquarian and Picturesque Tour in the Northern Counties of England* (1838) 'The lamp of Aladdin is found again ... Let me contemplate this worthy and mighty Architect as he deserves to be contemplated. His genius is his own, and vast as it is original ... When I quitted Newcastle in August I saw two hundred men at work, like a swarm of bees, in pulling down and rebuilding the theatre. When I returned, at the latter end of November, the theatre was rebuilt.'

[10] W. E. Gladstone: Diary Entry for 7th October, 1862 (see *Life of Gladstone*, John Morley Vol. 2, p. 78, 1903).

[11] *The Buildings of Britain* (Northumberland 1957, p. 249, Penguin Books).

and Nelson Street, must not be overlooked—although the defacements and demolitions already allowed in the two first named streets, and the dereliction in the two latter streets have resulted in a sad mutilation.

Those who came to Newcastle in the mid-nineteenth century with eyes to see, like Prime Minister Gladstone, and saw the new streets, wondered at their curving elegance and decoration and their then unparalleled width and spaciousness. Miss Martineau also finds herself puzzled in 1840:[12]

'... it remains to be inquired how the mind of the artist became fitted for the work he was now about to achieve. This no one seems able to explain—not even the man himself. It may be understood how a man of clever understanding and enterprising and placid temper, and strict integrity might become as perfect a man of business as Mr Grainger is ... But whence derived his powers as an artist remains a mystery. What his education was, we have seen, and how full has been the employment of his time since he left school. He had never been on the Continent, nor has he associated with artists except in consequences of his own enterprises, but he attributes much to a visit to Edinburgh many years ago. What he saw there gave him strong delight and a powerful impulse. He afterwards visited Dublin and London.'

The most probable answer is that at this time (as we have said in another chapter) Newcastle had had, within the fifty years before Grainger built his great streets, classical architects like William Newton, William Stokoe and David Stephenson, great silversmiths, designers and engravers on wood and copper, and painters on glass and canvas whose achievements make the period 1770-1840 Newcastle's golden age: and that to live in such a period encouraged those with natural taste engaged in building to build beautifully: but the natural taste had to be there. As Grainger said[13] he 'had great pleasure in giving them (his streets)

---

[12] *The Penny Magazine*, No. 516, 18th April, 1840.
[13] Evidence to the Cholera Commissioners 1854 reported in Town Council Proceedings 1854.

up to the town ... he had a taste for art and was not bound to decorate his houses in the manner the Commissioners had seen, but did it because it pleased him to do it, although the cost had probably been not less than £100,000'.

Grainger's contemporaries were in no doubt about the important part played by him in the design of his new streets. The *Newcastle Journal* of 8th June, 1837, referred to the most beautiful and elaborately designed side of Grey Street, including the Bank of England building, in terms which succeeding generations of architectural historians have chosen to ignore: '... the buildings just adverted to will complete the west side of Grey Street, the centre three ranges of which as well as the western half of Market Street and Grainger Street, it is but justice to say have been entirely designed in Mr Grainger's office by Mr Wardle under Mr Grainger's immediate directions.'

From the year 1838 until his death in 1861 there hovers over these later years of Richard Grainger a sense of frustration and anti-climax. The great work was over, and although much building was still to be done, his most important schemes were either successfully resisted by his opponents, or brought him personal ill fortune. All his efforts to extend Grainger Street beyond the Bigg Market and on to Neville Street were unsuccessful—and were not carried out until 1868, seven years after his death, and in a manner strikingly inferior to Grainger's Grainger Street; his proposal in 1838 to mitigate the inconvenience caused by the position of Stokoe's Moot Hall by building a new Law Court and Guildhall with Judge's Lodgings and Barristers' Retiring Rooms at a cost of £32,000, in the space between the top of Grey Street and Pilgrim Street was also defeated—although on this site Grainger succeeded in building for The Northumberland and Durham District Bank (now occupied by Lloyds Bank) one of the most beautiful buildings that even he ever built, rivalling the Bank of England building in the lower section of Grey Street.

But from 1839 onwards Grainger's life was dominated by the financial difficulties caused by his purchase from John Hodgson Hinde, of Elswick Hall, of the vast estate of Elswick extending to 800 acres for the price of £114,100.[14] At least £59,000 of this purchase price was provided by the Trustees of the Northumberland and Durham District Banking Company, William Backhouse and Thomas Mounsey, and loans and mortgages from all other sources (including John Clayton) totalled £103,942. It is quite clear therefore that Grainger embarked on this enormous enterprise with little or no money of his own, all his monies having up to 1838 been ploughed back into his central Newcastle development schemes. He had therefore—on a vaster scale even than before—to proceed by way of a complex of loans and mortgages to buy the property—and even more so to actually build upon it, so that at one point three creditors alone, the District Bank, Edward Backhouse, and Edward Richardson, were secured for just under £150,000.

Grainger, as always, saw the essence of Newcastle's problem. If the dignity of the new streets were to be maintained, the prosperity of the City must increase. The Elswick estate near the river must be the site of great industrial enterprises, new quays, new rail roads, new quarries, and higher up on the steep Elswick banks more and more houses would be needed, ranging from the substantial villas of Rye Hill to the long street of artisan dwellings bearing the names of Grainger's thirteen children—Henrietta Maria Street, Emily Street and so on—to house those either working in the new enterprises or in the new city itself.

What brought Grainger's intricate and towering edifice of credit crashing almost to disaster we do not know, owing to the destruction and loss of some of Grainger's most important papers, but by 22nd September, 1841, the position was so critical that Grainger left Newcastle to avoid possible arrest for debt, and his faithful lawyer and adviser is writing to him at Liverpool—

'I have ascertained beyond a doubt that Mr Richardson has no intention to purchase any part of the Elswick estate—his plan is to make a partial payment to the most pressing creditors —provided the large creditors will engage to give time for a period of two years ... No process against your person has

[14] Newcastle City Archives Office, Grainger Catalogue, Elswick parcel 12, No. 2.

reached the hands of the Sheriff ... in case any Creditor is obstinate a Bankruptcy must follow.'

The next day Clayton wrote:

'Mr Brown continues to press forward his proceedings and will oblige the Sheriff to sell everything. I continue to think you had better come here on Sunday. I can see you in Westgate Street at one o'clock. Another bill for £2,000 given to Mr Hinde is due.'

One week later Clayton writes to Grainger in Penrith:

'... there seems to be an increasing disposition on the part of the creditors to adopt Mr Richardson's suggestion and to allow you two years for payment, provided the whole of the proceeds of your property be placed under the control of Inspectors who shall ... allow you £300 p.a.

Of course it will be out of the question your continuing to live at Elswick on the income that is proposed to be allowed you.'

There are many letters of advice[15] written by Clayton to Grainger in this crisis advising on the best way to surmount it. In several letters Clayton has to stress that whilst he thinks he can get the creditors to agree to an arrangement whereby, although he will lose control of his properties until the creditors are paid and will have to live in only modest comfort on £300 a year and must leave Elswick Hall, he would not lose the legal ownership of the freeholds and bankruptcy would be avoided; nevertheless it is obvious that Grainger at one point felt the gravest difficulty in accepting his advice for Clayton has to write again with an undercurrent of impatience:

'It is now necessary that these matters be closed and that you should remove from Elswick not later than Tuesday next ... after Tuesday he will not permit you to use any of the furniture at Elswick ... There is no disposition on the part of any friends of yours to turn their backs on you unless you turn your back on yourself.'

[15] Reprinted in *Tyneside Classical* (John Murray, 1964) by Lyall Wilkes and Gordon Dodds.

Due entirely to John Clayton's skill and advice bankruptcy was avoided, and to the end Grainger continued to work and build, although his Inspectors were in control of his vast properties applying the rents to the paying off of creditors. But the difficulties were hidden from his townsfolk and there was neither the disgrace of bankruptcy nor indeed any public indignity at all suffered by the creator of the new Newcastle. Although now living at 5, Clayton Street West, instead of at Elswick Hall, he was very much until the day of his death the same vigorous and outwardly successful business man and builder he had always been, and was still the great figure in the Town he had been since the completion of the Royal Arcade in 1833.

On his death on 4th July, 1861, The Town Council Proceedings reported:

> 'Mr Richard Grainger, one of the greatest architects of his age, died suddenly today at his residence in West Clayton Street, Newcastle, aged sixty-four years. The event was soon made known and it was universally deplored. The minute bell of St Nicholas tolled at midday, whilst the shop keepers put up their shutters in a token of respect to the departed ... he was engaged up to half just ten o'clock in the morning issuing orders to his employees; at twelve he was suddenly taken ill; Dr Frost his medical attendant, was immediately called; but at half past twelve life was extinct. Disease of the heart was the cause of death.'

At his death Grainger still had forty-nine creditors who were owed £128,582 14s. 7d. and his personal estate amounted only to £16,913 2s. 6¾d. John Clayton completed his devoted service to Grainger's cause by not proving against Grainger's estate for his own mortgage debt of £30,000 and the arrears of interest on it, then already totalling over £4,400—a sacrifice of over £34,000 when that sum was worth many times what it is worth today. However, in the course of the next forty years after Grainger's death, rising land values and the consequent rise in rents, in conjunction with the skill of Clayton, transformed the situation, so that by 1901 when the last of the debts were able to be paid off, the total value of the Grainger Estate amounted then to £1,202,087.

When Richard Grainger died he could say as truly as Christopher Wren had said, 'If you seek my monument, look around'. Were he alive today he might add, as he contemplated a mutilated Eldon Square, 'but quickly, whilst it is still there'.

CHAPTER SIX

John Dobson

THE irony that has pursued John Dobson lies in the fact that his reputation with the general public is based upon work which he did not do, that recognition of the work he did do has grown only slowly because some of the best of it is hidden away in the Northumbrian countryside, and, thirdly, that the work he did in Newcastle is so often under threatened or actual demolition that it has been put about that it is not all that good after all. And if all this were not enough, the final irony is that his name has been commemorated by his own city, naming after him a new street which is a negation of every value to which he devoted his life.

He deserves better than this. From every account he seems to have been a modest unassuming man who devoted his life wholly to architecture and the arts. He was one of the original members of the Committee of the Northumberland Institution for The Promotion of the Fine Arts formed by T. M. Richardson in 1822 and such was his reputation for quiet integrity that not only does it seem probably correct, as his daughter said of him in her Memoir,[1] that he 'never exceeded an estimate and never had a legal dispute with a contractor', but his arbitration and advice was sought constantly to resolve disputes amongst architects, builders and artists in the town.

The 1885 Memoir by his daughter presents an interesting study of her psychology; for it is full of a scarcely veiled jealousy of Grainger's reputation who, she alleges, has been accorded a fame and success far beyond his merit, in contrast to Dobson who, the daughter claims, was the real author of the design of

---

[1] p. 35 Memoir of the late John Dobson M.R.I.B.A., by his daughter Margaret Jane Dobson, 1885.

the new town and whose name she laments is never now mentioned in connection with it. The picture of Grainger in The Memoir as one who had obtained success primarily due to the efforts of others (and mostly Dobson's) betrays no knowledge of the anxiety, unhappiness, and near financial breakdown which Grainger's efforts for the town had cost him (had she known the truth she might have shown less jealousy) and is an interesting and convincing testimony to Clayton's success in concealing Grainger's real position from his townsfolk.

Her claim that Dobson put forward plans for building a new town centre is correct. Dobson put these forward in 1824-25; and although the plan showed some similarities with Grainger's there were also important differences so that the daughter is wrong in saying 'it remained for another to take up his plans and to execute them, not without energy and enterprise'—the nearest to praise that Grainger is given in the memoir; but she is probably correct when she says of her father 'His nature was so entirely artistic as to unfit him to cope with the financial difficulties that beset great speculative schemes'. She ponders in the memoir on why there are those who obtain fame and success beyond their merit and those who obtain less than they deserve: 'it is no disparagement to others to remark that Mr Dobson's artistic hand is ever visible in the new town of Newcastle. And yet it is strange when we take into consideration the career of these two men—the architect with his genius, originating so great a scheme, throwing all his immense energy into the carrying out of the work, whose name is never remembered in connection with it; the other, the speculator and builder whose existence can never be forgotten so long as Newcastle stands and Grainger Street retains its name ... the curious faculty of succeeding, which some men possess, in contrast to the ability and genius of others, is here discernible.'

Indeed it would have been remarkable if within fifty years of Dobson planning and designing the new town it had been forgotten that he had done so. But this was not the truth. She says (and why did she not publish the documents?)—'From unpublished documents, Mr Dobson appears to have devoted much time and thought to the design of the façade of Grey Street ... so anxious was he that the scheme should be well carried out, that we find him with his usual absence of professional jealousy, sending in sketches and designs to be executed in Mr Grainger's office. Mr Wardle and Mr Walker were for some years Mr Grainger's office architects—both men of talent, who judically incorporated Mr Dobson's designs into their own work ... Mr Dobson furnished designs for a great portion of Grey Street, serving as a model to Mr Grainger's clerks for the rest.'

It is noteworthy that not even Miss Dobson claims here that all Grey Street was designed by Dobson, but this qualification is forgotten later when she states—'all the new streets were planned and levelled by Mr Dobson'. This proposition has the virtue of simplicity and from this proposition (starting from her complaint, that in 1885 no one would recognize Dobson as the designer), springs the modern belief that Dobson was the designer of all the new streets, Richard Welford in 1895[2] repeating her proposition word for word, and helping with others to establish the fiction; so that Professor Pevsner can say[3] in 1957 'Dobson himself clearly regarded Grey Street as the climax of his Newcastle work'.

The truth is a good deal more complicated and in the absence of the conclusive documents from Dobson's office and from Grainger's not entirely beyond dispute even now. What one can say is that after Jane Dobson's 1885 memoir, the further one gets away from 1837 (the completion year of the new streets) the more the simple story is told that Dobson is their sole creator; and the closer to 1837 the more insistently it is said that others played a greater part than Dobson, and the more prominence is given to the role played by Wardle and Walker.[4]

I have already in the preceding chapter quoted the crucial comment made by the Editor of the *Newcastle Journal* of 3rd June, 1837, when commenting on the beauty of the most elaborate western side of Grey Street—the Bank of England side—when he stated '... the buildings just adverted to will complete the west side of Grey Street, the centre three ranges of which as

[2] Richard Welford *Men of Mark 'twixt Tyne and Tweed*, Vol, II, page 83.
[3] *The Buildings of Northumberland* (Penguin Books), page 249.
[4] See for a fuller treatment of this problem of architectural attribution in Newcastle, *Tyneside Classical* by Lyall Wilkes and Gordon Dodds (Chapter 5).

well as the western half of Market Street and Grainger Street, it is but justice to say have been entirely designed in Mr Grainger's office by Mr Wardle under Mr Grainger's immediate directions'. The same extract also states that Wardle designed the south side of Shakespeare Street and that the north side was designed by John and Benjamin Green during their designs for the Theatre Royal erected in 1837. There was no dissent from these statements in the succeeding issues of the *Newcastle Journal* when there was greater interest in who deserved the credit for the beauty of the new streets than at any subsequent time, and when all the claimants for the honour were alive and working in the town.

Moreover, on 21st March, 1868, a letter was published in the *Newcastle Daily Chronicle* signed 'VERITAS' which strikingly confirmed the 1837 view set out above. This letter was part of correspondence which had resulted from a *Newcastle Daily Chronicle* attribution of too much architectural credit to Grainger personally and stated—

> 'The Butcher and Green Markets with the block of houses enclosing them were designed by the late Mr John Dobson who also designed the portion of the East side of Grey Street which reaches from Shakespeare Street to Mosley Street.
>
> The late John and Benjamin Green designed the Theatre and surrounding block ... all the rest of the new streets, including part of Grey Street, Grainger Street, Market Street, Clayton Street, etc. etc., were designed by the late Mr John Wardle. The Central Exchange was not Mr Dobson's design but Mr Wardle's assisted by Mr George Walker.'

All the above in no way lessens Dobson's status or his leading role in creating the new architectural beauty of Newcastle. As the designer of Eldon Square, St Mary's Place, St Thomas' Church, part of Grey Street, The Academy of Arts in Blackett Street and the Royal Arcade, in addition to the Central Station (the portico was Dobson's design but was not built until 1863 after his retirement under the supervision of Thomas Prosser the Railway Company's own architect), as well as the new markets in the town and many fine buildings since demolished—he does not need the attribution to him of work which he did not do—

(his daughter even claiming in her memoir that Dobson designed Leazes Terrace and Crescent which were in fact built by Grainger to the designs of Thomas Oliver). Moreover, as well as being acknowledged the leading architect of his time in Newcastle, because his interests and activities reached out into other arts— he was a fine watercolourist in his own right and exhibited frequently at T. M. Richardson's exhibitions—he was second only to T. M. Richardson in his influence on art in Newcastle from about 1822 until his death. And as a designer of homes for the merchants and iron masters grown rich with the growth of ship building, engineering and the coal trade on Tyneside, Dobson achieved in these houses a new airy elegance combined with a monumentality based on severely classical forms that makes his contribution to the evolution of that peculiarly English art form —the country house—totally distinctive.

Dobson was born on 9th December, 1787, in the building which is now the Pineapple Inn in High Chirton, North Shields. As a young child he showed an exceptional gift for drawing and whilst still only eleven years of age was appointed 'Honorary Draftsman' to a celebrated local damask weaver, a Mr McClashan, and executed designs for him. At the age of fifteen he was placed as a pupil with the leading architect-builder in Newcastle, David Stephenson, designer of the classical round Church of All Saints and of the original Theatre Royal which stood in the then new Mosley Street. Whilst a pupil of Stephenson he also became a pupil of Boniface Moss, an Italian refugee who taught him painting. John Martin was a fellow pupil of Moss at this time learning the technique of enamel painting on glass just over twenty years after the departure of William and Mary Beilby from Newcastle.

By 1810, at the age of twenty-three, his studies with Stephenson completed, Dobson (like Bewick before him), decided that before trying to establish himself in Newcastle he would go to London and improve his knowledge of art in general. He sought out John Varley who was then at the height of his popularity as a watercolourist and who attempted unsuccessfully to rebuff Dobson in his attempt to become a pupil. So busy was Varley at this time that Dobson's lessons with him had to begin at five in the morning but a friendship sprang up between them that lasted until Varley's death and in a short time Dobson was working all the day in Varley's studio. A testimony to their intimacy was a picture entitled 'Dobson's dream' which Varley exhibited at the Royal Academy. Dobson had had a vivid dream of woods, water and buildings and had immediately on waking drawn his dream landscape. Varley had made his picture out of Dobson's pencil sketch.

It is not certain how long Dobson remained in London but it cannot have been for much more than a year, because by 1810 or 1811 his first commissions were being undertaken and amongst the very first was the task of assisting Sir Charles Monck in the designing of Belsay Hall—an even more severely classical and rigorous building than any which Dobson himself designed.[5] One of Dobson's earliest and most successful smaller villas is Prestwick Lodge (1815), a small three bay villa of great beauty. Amidst hundreds of design commissions, and excluding all mention of the large variety of restorations and alterations to churches, houses, and schools, the following examples are given only to indicate some of the immense variety of the original work on which he was to be engaged for the rest of his life.

In 1817 Sandyford Park (now called Nazareth House), in 1818 the artificial lake at Bolam, and Doxford Hall near Embleton; 1822, Morpeth Gaol (now the Courthouse, Morpeth); 1823, Angerton Hall near Hartburn, an exercise in the Tudor and Gothic style, and in the same year the classical Mitford Hall with its Greek Doric entrance. In the same year Dobson completed the exterior classical transformation of Trollap's Guildhall in Newcastle; 1824-1826, Eldon Square; 1825, Nunykirk Hall one of his classical masterpieces, and the Church of St Thomas the Martyr, Barras Bridge, Newcastle on Tyne; 1826, the Lying-in-Hospital, New Bridge Street (now BBC Newcastle Headquarters); 1827, St Mary's Place; 1828, Northern Academy of Arts and Longhirst Hall, Morpeth—another classical masterpiece; 1831-32, Royal Arcade; 1832, Meldon Park; 1835,

---

[5] I am grateful to Mr Bruce Allsopp, who has recently inspected the original designs for Linden Hall, for the information that this house (1812), hitherto attributed to Dobson was in fact designed by Sir Charles Monck.

Grainger Market, and designing East side of Grey Street; 1835-41 Beaufront Castle, Dobson's most ambitious exercise in the Tudor and Gothic style; 1839, Newcastle General Cemetery (now Jesmond Cemetery); 1849-1850, Central Railway Station, with a fine colonnade and portico, which as mentioned previously was to Dobson's design but not built by him; 1857-59, Terraces of Neo-classical houses built at Whitby for George Hudson, 'the Railway King'; 1858, Clayton Memorial Church (Jesmond Parish Church), a memorial to John Clayton's brother, Richard Clayton first Master of St Thomas's Church.

The above mentioned works are only a few of the hundreds of commissions he carried out in addition to preparing his plans in 1824-25 for a new town centre to be built on the same open spaces that Grainger later exploited. In addition he carried out such difficult and dangerous operations as underpinning and supporting in 1832 the famous lantern tower of St Nicholas Cathedral in imminent danger of collapse. During his last years he spent much time creating new and secure foundations for a new Lambton Castle, the old Castle having had to be pulled down because of the subsidence of the earth due to the colliery workings underneath: Dobson was compelled to build up the empty seams with solid continuous beds of masonry before any building could begin, the principal walls having in some places to be carried down to the depth of fifteen feet below the cellar floors. The underpinning of the walls alone took six years. A less exacting commission was executing in 1855 Ruskin's suggestion to roof-in the courtyard of Wallington Hall. Dobson designed the arcaded walls, the pillars and spandrels of which were painted over by William Bell Scott, Pauline Trevelyan, and Ruskin himself.

It may not be without interest in view of the suggestions now being made about Newcastle's Old Town Hall to realize that one of the few matters on which Dobson expressed himself in terms approaching anger was the 1863 siting of John Johnson's building. Dobson commented that it hid the cathedral and had spoiled a potentially wonderful architectural prospect down the old curving Bigg Market from its northern point in Grainger Street, which could have taken in at the south end not only the view of the Cathedral tower, but the Castle and Black Gate. He proposed that instead of the Town Hall being sited there, the site should have been left open and a street vista created which could rival the parallel Grey Street. It is a pity that his advice was not taken.

Although Dobson's architectural versatility allowed him to build in the Gothic and Tudor style whenever his clients so wished, a study of his life's work makes it clear that the classical style was his first and last love. He was fortunate in that because fashion in building in Northumberland (like in most other things), lagged about fifteen or twenty years behind London, this saved him from the necessity to build many a house which was an unhappy synthesis of the English Cathedral and the Norman Castle, and allowed him (and other architects) in Northumberland, to go on building plain decent Georgian houses until the 1840s; and even when he did build in the Gothic style and the main house today appears somewhat intimidating, his lightness of touch ensured that there were charming lodges and smaller estate houses built in a delicate and slightly Gothicized style. These can be seen all over Northumberland especially around Matfen, Cheeseburn Grange and Milbourne.

But Dobson's particular importance was that he succeeded in adapting the Greek forms of architecture to the successful designing of houses large and small, to shops and streets, to schools—and even to Railway stations. His Monkwearmouth Railway Station (now disused) is a particular gem of a building; and when it was suggested that a style other than classical was the style most suitable for railway stations he was sufficiently aroused to reject the suggestion in one of his rare speeches.[6]

The country houses of great beauty and individuality which he designed in the classical style are too little known, chiefly because these houses are not so large that they can continue to be lived in only by opening them to the public (indeed Nunnykirk and Meldon Park are still lived in by members of the same family that commissioned Dobson to build), yet are large enough to be hidden from view by parkland and wood. Recognition of

[6] From *Civil Engineering and Architect's Journal* reported in the *Yorkshire Gazette*, 6th January, 1849.

their architectural importance is growing[7] and a complete study of them by an architectural historian is much overdue.

The outstanding characteristics of the most important Dobson country houses are the magnificently worked and veined golden coloured sandstone—the blocks of stone sometimes weighing many tons—the Corinthian or Ionic pillared entrance portico, the elegant staircases with beautiful iron work balustrades, worked with classical Greek motifs, dividing to form separate stairways up on to an upper gallery extending around the whole upper floor, with an iron balustrade of the same design forming the upper gallery rail: and above the gallery is the roof of the open hall with its domed ceiling and glass centrepiece. There is frequently too, as at Nunnykirk and Longhirst as part of the ground floor design a graceful curved or bow end at one side of the house.

At Longhirst Hall the gigantic Corinthian pillars have been given a pediment—which some may think is a mistake: but what makes Longhirst unique (and this is not too strong a word) is that the oval hall (illustrated) and the Ionic columns, and the floor and walls are all of naked stone superbly cut—a triumph of the stone mason's art. At Nunnykirk the design is similar save that the hall and all its detail is in fine plasterwork, and the exterior of the house is remarkable for the strong horizontal rustication. Meldon Park has an Ionic Porch (illustrated) and Mark Girouard tells us that Dobson's estimate for the house still survives; it is dated June 26th, 1832, and was for £7,188 1s. 11d., not including the stables.

These classical country houses give the best indication of Dobson's high achievement as an architect. But Pevsner and many others have given high praise to his town work, such as the now half demolished Eldon Square; and his Churches— especially St Thomas's—have a soaring grace. In 1859 when he was seventy-two years of age he was elected first President of the newly formed Northern Architectural Association, retired from active work in 1863, and went to live for a time at Ryton. He died however on 8th January, 1865, aged seventy-seven years at his home in New Bridge Street (which was on the site of what

[7] See two articles on John Dobson's Northumbrian Houses by Mark Girouard in *Country Life* of 16th and 24th February, 1966.

is now called the 'Dobson Suite' of the Oxford Galleries). He left a comfortable fortune of just under £16,000 and his executors were his daughter Margaret Jane Dobson and his son-in-law Sydney Smirke, a noted London architect and younger brother of Sir Robert Smirke RA.

'The best of philosophic and poetic natures, a man of the truest genius'
                      Dante Gabriel Rossetti
                      on William Bell Scott.

'A frozen Keats'
      Edmund Gosse on William Bell Scott.

'Now all the cherished secrets of my heart—
Now all my hidden hopes are turned to sin.
Part of my life is dead, part sick, and part
Is all on fire within'
                      Christina Rossetti.

'Besides, 'twas God's progressive plan
Before we straightened up to Man,
The instincts ruled in place of mind;
And even now, although consigned
The late born reasoning soul to serve,
They obey the Sympathetic Nerve—
Inherited anatomies still
Ordering our acts against our will.'
                      William Bell Scott.

'Dead on the breast of the dying year,
Poet and Painter and friend, thrice dear
   For love of the suns long set, for love
Of song that sets not with sunset here'
                Algernon Charles Swinburne
                (from Memorial Verses on the Death of
                William Bell Scott[1]).

[1] Published in the *Athenaeum*, 28th February, 1891.

CHAPTER SEVEN

William Bell Scott

MOST men achieve oblivion on merit; some, like William Bell Scott, have it thrust upon them. To excel in both painting and poetry is dangerous to a reputation in either—as Dante Gabriel Rossetti also found—such excess of talent being regarded as dangerous and even as indicating a lack of high seriousness and respect for art. Yet in the case of Bell Scott, it must be admitted, his life and work and character troubles the mind even after a hundred years.

A man so fascinating to women that two as remarkable as Christina Rossetti and Alice Boyd condemned themselves to die unmarried because they could not marry him; who spent most of the last thirty years of his life with Alice Boyd who was so frequently a guest under his matrimonial roof that she became, as did Christina, the personal friend of the wife he treated with a courteous indifference that rarely faltered; who wrote an autobiography in places impressively honest, self-questioning and generous, yet elsewhere displays a sour indifference to the feelings of others, especially his wife's, and a jealousy of Gabriel Rossetti, his 'dearest and most attached friend', that made him depict him in a sometimes ridiculous light.

Gabriel Rossetti, like many other men of genius, was sometimes ridiculous, and must have appeared especially so to a Scottish agnostic and rationalist follower of Voltaire; but it is not the act of a friend to use the knowledge of failings which friendship brings, to hint at insanity and to make a dead friend ridiculous (whether what is written is true or not), even although elsewhere in the book high tribute is paid. Perhaps in the last resort his behaviour was characteristic of the moral obtuseness sometimes shown by really clever men. Most of the autobiography was written in 1877, Rossetti died in 1882, the autobiography was revised until Scott's death in 1890 and was published in 1892. And the book instead of crowning his achievements helped to consign his poetry and his painting to an obscurity they certainly do not deserve, and so incensed the admirers of Rossetti —who tended in any event to excuse even the inexcusable—that reports of the book losing nothing in the telling, caused such grief to Christina, that after a totally frustrate and life long love for the man himself, she could never bring herself to read it.

Few human beings contrive to live without serious fault and without inflicting, consciously or unconsciously, pain and suffering upon others. Judgement in such matters is always difficult, and sometimes (especially in modern biography) verges on impertinence. Judgement is especially difficult in the case of this physically impressive and charming arch-fiend from the north, with his unnerving intense blue eyes, looking out from under the sharply angled bushy black eyebrows.

The problem he presents is illustrated by his treatment of his wife in the Autobiography. Pauline, Lady Trevelyan is described as 'my never-to-be-forgotten good angel'. His first meeting with Alice Boyd is described as 'the day of days', the beginning of 'the perfect friendship, the ambition of my life' with the woman who had 'the most interesting face and voice I had ever heard or seen'. On the twenty-first anniversary of his meeting with Miss Boyd he wrote a moving sonnet containing the lines—

> 'Your smile is still as bright as long ago,
> We still are gathering shells on life's sea shore,
>   We still can walk like children hand in hand,
> Friendship and love beside us ever more.'

But for the wife who suffered his long absences, kept his house for over forty years, helped to look after him, made friends with his women friends, there is no poetry and no praise. The nearest to praise she receives is the comment that she is 'without jealousy', but he describes his marriage as the 'most imprudent step in life' and says that his wife was 'the most difficult of human creatures to understand'. He must have known how hurtful these references would be to his wife, yet this is the man of whom Alice Boyd wrote—'I have known him deprived of sleep by the thought that perhaps a spoken or written word of his might hurt the feelings of a friend', and the editor of the Autobiography says of the book, 'A wise and charitable soul makes itself felt in every chapter'.

Of Christina Rossetti there is in the two volumes scarcely more than a passing and very casual mention, although one so often in the company of her brothers would frequently see her, and although she had stayed with him and his wife in Newcastle for several weeks in 1858 and spent the summer of 1868 with him at Miss Boyd's Penkill Castle, and each had frequently been entertained at the other's London home. He was not unaware of the injury that autobiographical writing can inflict upon others, for this published work is the successor to his first autobiography written between 1852 and 1854 (he met Christina for the first time in 1847) which he burnt in 1877, saying it was written when he was 'unable to see what was fit and what was unfit for possible preservation'. 'To write one's mental history is too difficult as well as too dreadful ... We go about with so many deceptive coverings that a sincere attempt at self-portraiture in writing is like walking into the street naked, and is only likely to frighten our neighbours.'

The only explanation of the curious mixture of kindness and callousness, perception and insensitivity characterizing the Autobiography is, I think, that Scott as a radical rationalist with a life long contempt for Victorian humbug must have felt himself at the age of sixty-seven under a compulsion to tell the truth—at least about the less dangerous topics he committed himself to in his second Autobiography. 'My work is not Art for Art's sake but truth for truth's sake', he wrote. He forgot that important as the truth is in public affairs, in writing about private affairs and relationships (which is gossip merely), the question to be asked by a sensible man is whether the truth serves any purpose important enough to counterbalance the pain it will cause, and secondly (before he dispenses with the humane hypocrisies that render human relationships tolerable), whether the truth he sees may not be only partial truth, or even less than that. Unless these questions are asked and answered 'truth telling' becomes a form of self-indulgence.

In the end, the book, like the man himself, remains largely

inexplicable. One has to accept it as such, and as a fascinating record of literary and artistic life in early and Mid-Victorian England by a man who had known Leigh Hunt, Sir Walter Scott, George Eliot, Clough, Benjamin Haydon, the whole Pre-Raphaelite world, Carlyle and Tennyson, and in Newcastle had talked to and entertained the elder Richardson, Carmichael, Robert Bewick and many others—and yet who lived on until the days of the early motor car.

He was born in Edinburgh on 12th September, 1811, the son of a prosperous engraver and printer who, he writes, had no interest in anything but 'business, religion and the state of his pulse'. Almost his first recollection is of soldiers returning home to Edinburgh after the battle of Waterloo. His elder brother was David Scott, a painter of historical and allegorical pictures of rare ability, and a man of great integrity who refused to paint the portraits and the landscapes that would have brought him success, and who—as the portrait of his brother in this book shows—was a painter of great power.

In Edinburgh Scott divided his time between learning the art of engraving to please his father, assisting in his father's business, learning painting under Sir William Allan in the Antique Class at the Trustee's Gallery, publishing his first poems in Edinburgh's literary magazines, and exhibiting his first picture, a landscape, at one of the earliest Scottish Academy Exhibitions on the Mound in 1833-34. He became a well known figure in Edinburgh's art circles with a little circle of friends amongst whom was the Reverend John Thomson of Duddingston with whom he sat whilst Thomson painted the landscapes that are now increasingly admired. He had a not very encouraging interview with Sir Walter Scott about his poetry, when Scott advised the young man not to write in blank verse and not to try to emulate Milton but to write in rhyme with a more modest aim.

The precocious and ambitious Scott left Edinburgh to try his luck as poet and engraver in 1837 in London at the age of twenty-six. When he left Edinburgh he had with him the draft of the poem Rosabell which Rossetti later so admired, and his long poem 'The Year of the World' was already forming in his mind. He quickly became disillusioned with the artificiality, triviality and commercialism of London's artistic life, and makes a shrewd comment on the difference between the intellectual worlds of the two capitals. 'He (Sir Walter Scott) was not the literary man by profession but a gentleman. His interests sprang not from books but from life. It was the same with all the Scotch literati, they were Lords of Sessions, professors, men of fortune; the ball had been at their feet from boyhood. How different it was in London! None of the literary men and few of the poets were in a similar position. They were all living hand to mouth, working in a groove or in a comparatively obscure public office like Charles Lamb, whose writing, like himself, was essentially middle class. Hazlitt was a noble fellow in his way but altogether uncertain in habits and position; and with John Scott, Peacock, Reynolds, Leigh Hunt, Keats, we ascend to the pure air of genius, but get no higher in the social scale.' But in London Scott found that work of the highest literary distinction did not compensate for lack of social position—as it would have in the more severe intellectual atmosphere of Edinburgh.

His main friendships in London were with Leigh Hunt, Richard Dadd, W. J. Linton, Augustus Egg and Frith. He was taken to the Garrick Club 'where I first saw the Landseers, Douglas Jerrold, Blanchard and others who seemed all preternaturally shrewd and sharp, and initiated in some mental freemasonry I could not enter'. Marrying Letitia Norquoy with a singular lack of enthusiasm, a settled income now became a necessity. In any event London, in spite of friendships made, was only deepening his sense of personal and artistic isolation. He had had two pictures rejected by the Academy and the British Institution, the publisher who had accepted designs from him for the Illustrated Book of Ballads had gone bankrupt, and although his entry for the Government sponsored competition for Fresco paintings for the new Houses of Parliament was not amongst the winners, it did result in Scott being offered one of the new appointments being created by the Board of Trade—a Mastership in one of the several new Schools of Design—one of which was being established in Newcastle.

These new schools—as Scott ironically wrote were—'to teach the working class, who could not hold a pencil to create new decorative designs, and even begin new trades' and were a singularly enlightened if muddled idea. The emphasis was on the practical application of Art to Industry. Scott was forbidden to teach drawing or colour or to admit any student intending to make art his profession, and drawing from the human figure was prohibited. As Scott said later, writing of the general distrust of art in England, 'The Government dare not come before Parliament acknowledging the establishment of Schools of Art'. But Scott made his own rules independent of Somerset House and taught drawing and landscape, and other forbidden subjects. The indefatigable John Dobson was the Chairman of the first meeting which Scott addressed in Newcastle in February 1844 on the aims and methods of the new school. The terms were two shillings a month payable in advance for classes in drawing and ornamental design, Landscape Drawing, Geometry, Perspective and Projection, and in the preliminary announcement 'The attention of the Manufacturers of Tyne and Wear is respectfully directed to the Classes conducted by the Government Teacher, Mr W. B. Scott'. The old North of England Society for the Promotion of the Fine Arts, which had been created by T. M. Richardson in 1822 but which had been taken over from him in the late 1830s was now almost moribund, and Scott inherited from it a large number of plaster casts and other materials for art education. 'Mr Richardson, a really admirable landscape painter, the father of many Richardsons—wrote to the Board of Trade that the School of Design was taking the bread from them, and the Board remonstrated with me for doing what I had actually been appointed to do.'

For twenty years Scott was to prove an inspiring art teacher in Newcastle. Thomas Dixon the Sunderland cork cutter to whom Ruskin addressed the letters published under the title 'Time and Tide by Weare and Tyne', the man who discovered the unknown Whitman's 'Leaves of Grass' (sending it to Scott, who sent it to William Rossetti who made Whitman's reputation), confessed that 'he owed all the great blessings which had enriched his life to Scott';[2] and there were many others on Tyneside who would have said the same including Dixon's friend, Joseph Skipsey, the pitman poet. Scott's Autobiography reveals

[2] *Christina Rossetti* by Lona Mosk Packer, p. 419 (Cambridge University Press and University of California Press, 1963).

the respect and even the humility with which he approached working people. All his life he felt the fascination of watching practical skills at work—whether it was the stone mason or the ploughman or any other—and in this respect, as in others, he was the first pre-Raphaelite long before the founding of the Brotherhood in 1848 and long before Madox Brown, Ruskin and Gabriel Rossetti in the 1850s began to teach the mysteries of art—by then a Pre-Raphaelite article of faith—to artisans in Camden Town and at the Working Men's College in Red Lion Square, London.

Newcastle and the North fascinated Scott after his disillusion with London's art and life 'A hard and precarious life creates noble natures'. 'In Jarrow the dust of antique civilization is blown in the visitor's face, mixed with the grimy powder of the pit-heap, and the large strong serviceable women, old and young, running with their lumps of dough to the common oven in the middle of the village, look like the tradition of a thousand years, when Bede might see them from his cell when he ventured to open his little casement ... the fishing villages again show the same types of men and women.'

As to Newcastle in the 1840s—'a mixture of almost medieval tenements with the newest splendidly built streets ... great stone built streets and detached buildings in the "Italian style". There still existed an aristocratic quarter; a long quiet street or two, removed equally from the busy trading thoroughfares and the brand new rows of well built houses, with modest balconies and old-fashioned little porches, where the remaining county gentlefolk made a community to themselves as they had done for centuries ... there was an intermediate class equally interesting ... who had an ancestral connection with the business of the town ... Some of these in whose hands still existed shops of a common character, were very cultivated; more so than the "county people" who had no special call to know anything. Amongst these were the Hancocks, of whom Albany ... became my dear friend, as well as his younger brother John, the first man who made bird stuffing at once a science and an art.'

His portraits of Newcastle artists blow away the cobwebs of a hundred years. He tells of how when Carmichael 'sold a picture in London one year, nothing would stop him; he would leave the provinces, cut out Stanfield, make his fortune great and his name immortal'. There was only one drawback—the frightful boredom of the correct Londoners. Carmichael told Scott, 'I could not stand the dullness of a social evening—I couldn't stand it—so at last I started up and danced a hornpipe by myself; but I was soon stopped off, for instead of anybody else following my example, they looked at each other as if they thought I'd gone mad'. Scott attended the farewell presentation to Carmichael when he left Newcastle—between £200-£300 was subscribed for his silver presentation. 'The Vicar made a flowery speech and upset the painter by his allusion to uprooting the tree from its native soil.' Scott records that the mistress of the hotel in which the presentation was made was 'a handsome young widow, and when she was handed forward to examine the silver plate, Carmichael, who had quite recovered his spirits, made a dash at her, seized her round the neck and gave her such a sounding kiss as dispersed the company in a burst of laughter'. There are equally vivid pictures of Robert Bewick, the older Richardson, Luke Clennell's son, William Martin (John Martin's mad brother), and many others.

Although he was happier in Newcastle than he had been in London, with work to do which he enjoyed, the sense of isolation persisted. This feeling had been increased by the world turning its back on his first two volumes of verse, 'Hades' published in 1836, and 'The Year of The World' published in 1846. They were he said 'printed, published, still-born'.

But on 25th November, 1847, a letter arrived with a London postmark, bearing the address 50, Charlotte Street, which changed Scott's whole life. It was from a nineteen-year-old youth praising Rosabell and the 1846 volume—'a finer, more dignitous, a more deeply thoughtful production, a work that is more truly a *work*—has seldom, indeed, shed its light upon me. To me I can truly say that it revealed "some depth unknown, some inner life unlived".' It was signed Gabriel Charles Rossetti.[3] Within a month of receiving Rossetti's letter he visited London to bask at once in the affectionate admiration of the whole Rossetti family. For the rest of his life he would have his place as an

---

[3] He did not call himself Dante Gabriel Rossetti until later.

inner member of the Pre-Raphaelite circle. His years of artistic isolation were over.

In his Autobiography Scott describes his first meeting with the Rossetti family at their home in Charlotte Street. 'By the window was a high narrow reading-desk, at which stood writing a slight girl with a serious regular profile, dark against the pallid wintry light without. This most interesting to me of the two inmates turned on my entrance, made the most formal and graceful curtsey, and resumed her writing ...' This beautiful and graceful young woman was Christina Rossetti.

In one of the great biographies[4] of this century, Lona Mosk Packer has traced through external evidence and the evidence in Christina's poetry, her life long love for Bell Scott. The book is utterly convincing and leaves no more to be said. It is a terrible story and brought Christina great suffering. It was the source also of some of her greatest poetry.

At this first meeting in 1847 Christina was about to become engaged to James Collinson, shortly to be one of the original Brotherhood of seven, the only one to make no mark at all, and a man so dull that the wonder is not that the engagement was broken in 1850 by Christina but that it ever took place at all. Christina met with no further proposal until Charles Cayley's proposal of 1862—yet it was between 1850 and 1862 that her most passionate and despairing love poetry was written. In editing his sister's poetry after her death, and in writing about his sister, William Michael Rossetti attributes this despair to her encounters with Collinson and Cayley. The explanation is as unconvincing as Mrs Packer's book is convincing.

Had Bell Scott behaved from this first meeting with the Rossettis in December 1847, as a married man, or given any indication at all of his marriage, Christina would have steeled herself even more to prevent herself becoming emotionally involved. It tormented her enough that the man to whom she became engaged in 1848 filled her with an increasing impatience as the months went by. But for two and a half years, despite his visits to London, the Rossetti family knew nothing of his marriage.

[4] *Christina Rossetti* by Lona Mosk Packer, Cambridge University Press and University of California Press, 1963.

Christina was attracted (as were so many women) to this 'demon from the North', and it was not until Gabriel's visit to stay with Scott in Newcastle in September 1850 that Scott was discovered to be married.[5] Gabriel wrote 'We had not hitherto known distinctly whether Scott was a married man or bachelor'; Christina in May or June 1850 had broken off her engagement and this news of Scott's impossible position came as a staggering blow.

For many years she was torn between the idea of totally rejecting his friendship and never seeing him (which idea faltered as soon as he began to neglect her, as over long periods he did), or of accepting as much of his friendship as he deigned to offer, always remembering that for a woman of her strict principles even a limited emotional friendship with a married man was something to be deplored, and was the cause to her of bitter self-recrimination and reproach. In some of her poems the contemplation of a frustrated life which she saw clearly ahead, is accompanied by a craving for physical love which makes her poetry at times almost too painful to read. It was not until the middle 1860s that her feelings, with the years, became more resigned to what the future offered, and enabled her to extract even a troubled enjoyment from her acceptance of Miss Boyd's invitation to spend the summer of 1868 at Penkill Castle, Ayrshire, which since 1859 had been Scott's summer home, sometimes with and sometimes without his wife. To the end of Scott's life she maintained a fairly close and friendly relationship with both Mrs Scott and Miss Boyd as well as with Scott himself.

David Scott died on 5th March, 1849, at the age of forty-three, a great loss to Scottish painting. In 1850 Bell Scott, in the midst of his work at Newcastle, wrote the Memoir of his brother which was reviewed by Pauline, Lady Trevelyan in the *Scotsman*. Scott had not then met her, but this review helped to pave the way for her eventual invitation to visit Wallington in 1854. In that year his third volume of poetry 'Poems by a Painter' was published and he sent a copy to Sir Walter Trevelyan and Lady Pauline.

Through her writings in the Edinburgh literary magazines,

[5] The same, pp. 59-60.

Lady Pauline would have been known to him even before she reviewed his book. Before her marriage to Sir Walter in 1835 at the age of nineteen (Sir Walter was then exactly twice her age) she had been Pauline Jermyn, the daughter of a Cambridgeshire clergyman, a girl who delighted in learned discussion with her father's friends and even then showed such an extraordinary intelligence and personality that it must have been apparent that she would become one of the most remarkable women of her generation, as she did, before dying piteously young. In 1833 Walter Trevelyan then heir to the baronetcy and the estates, a mineral collector, a hypochondriac and an expert geologist, had met her at the Cambridge meeting of the British Association for the Advancement of Science. A man who rarely smiled, a pamphleteering teetotaller, it has been said[6] that 'by the age of thirty-six his emotions had begun to resemble the fossils to which he was so devoted', and since (like Scott's own father) he studiously refrained from any activity calculated to increase his pulse rate, he might justifiably be thought to be for ever debarred from courtship.

Lady Pauline was small in stature, hazel eyed, 'light as a feather and as quick as a kitten'[7] and amazingly frank and direct in speech for her day. We do not know what effect she had on Walter Trevelyan's pulse rate but we do know that he married her within two years of their first meeting. The Trevelyans' first eleven years were spent mostly travelling abroad and although it is difficult to visualize the stolid Walter at ease in Roman or Paris society it must be stressed that Pauline's parties were never frivolous although doubtless enjoyable. They were the means by which she could meet and talk to men of learning and achievement and participate in the only kind of conversation that interested her, so that even 'the scientists who called on the taciturn husband stayed on to enjoy the sparkling conversation of the gay little wife'.[8] She emulated Edward Lear and travelled through Greece on mule, her articles on her travels appearing in Blackwood's Magazine and Chambers Journal, and the

[6] 'Without the Passion of Love' by Osbert Wyndham Hewett (*The Listener*, 23rd January, 1958).
[7] William Bell Scott's 'Autobiographical Notes', Volume 2, page 3.
[8] See again Osbert Wyndham Hewett's article.

talented watercolours and drawings she made of her travels were not only highly praised by Ruskin and the Pre-Raphaelites, but can be studied today in the British Museum.

In 1846 Walter succeeded to the title, and both decided that their preference was for Wallington as their permanent home rather than Nettlecombe Court in Somerset. Both loved Scotland and the Border country—she particularly was fond of Edinburgh where she was held in high regard in literary circles, and Sir Walter became a formidable authority—as he did on most things to which he set his mind—on Border Ballads and History. They settled down in Northumberland and a constant stream of the intelligentsia of their day made pilgrimages to Pauline—Sir Walter devoting more and more time to the ordering of his estates and to his geological interests which frequently took him away from home for long periods.

Between Pauline and Ruskin there grew a friendship which lasted until her death, and Ruskin, Effie and John Millais stayed at Wallington on their ill-starred journey north in 1853. It was Sir Walter who first awakened Algernon Swinburne's interest in the Border Ballads and songs, and from about 1854 the seventeen-year-old poet, already an excitable oddity against the background of the Northumbrian landscape, frequently rode over from his home at nearby Capheaton during the holidays from Eton.

Of Lady Pauline, Scott writes 'the face was one that would be charming to some and distasteful to others ... as the observer was sympathetic or otherwise'. Within seconds of their first meeting Scott became a fervent sympathizer for life, recording that she liked his plain speech and congratulating himself that, Sir Walter 'a man of few words and many unacknowledged peculiarities', was then away from Wallington so that he had Lady Pauline to himself for a few days. From 1854 until 1864 the three centres of Scott's life were the School in Newcastle, Wallington, and the Rossetti household in London.

That Scott grew fond of Pauline, 'his never-to-be-forgotten good angel' is plain from many things, not least by his dislike of those men such as Swinburne and Ruskin who also had influence over her. 'With all Lady Trevelyan's discrimination in art ... she had not risen above the Turner mania: and the exponent of Turner, Mr Ruskin, I soon found, held an overpowering influence over her ... his overpowering passion in talk as in writing was a determination to find out qualities no one else could see, and to contradict or ignore those evident to everyone else.'

Under Scott's influence, she now began to commission paintings from the Pre-Raphaelites who, as Scott's friends, were invited to stay at Wallington—Holman Hunt, William Morris and Gabriel Rossetti amongst them. Woolner stayed, and she commissioned from him the sculpture which still stands in the central hall. After Dobson had carried out Ruskin's suggestion and roofed in the central courtyard, Scott was entrusted with the task of painting scenes from Northumberland history on its walls, the figures in them being nearly all portraits of recognizable local personalities. John Clayton appears as the centurion with the rod in the painting of the Building of the Roman Wall, in The Descent of The Danes upon the coast near Tynemouth, Lady Trevelyan is the highest female figure on the cliffs, and in the Grace Darling picture the woman on the ship is Alice Boyd.

These murals occupied Scott for weeks at a time at Wallington between 1856 and 1861 during which times he delighted in Pauline's company. As for Sir Walter, he is revealed by Scott as a comic character fit to stand by the side of Sir William Eden and Sir George Sitwell in any English gallery of eccentric aristocratic genius. 'His want of humour and imagination' writes Scott, 'was only perceptible as a secret amusement to her.' One is not so sure of the want of humour.

Sir Walter, author of the pamphlets 'On the Alcohol and Opium Trades' and 'On the Purity of Beer and Cider', inheriting one of the rarest and best cellars in England with wines dating back to the middle of the eighteenth century, left every bottle to Dr B. W. Richardson, his brother in temperance agitation, to be employed—as his will put it—'for scientific purposes'. Under Lady Pauline's rule however wine was invariably to be seen on the table at Wallington. When a visitor aghast at the spurned richness of his cellar offered to buy some rare port at a handsome price, Sir Walter firmly declined saying 'No, I mean to have the whole carried out some day and emptied into the Wansbeck.' When to Sir Walter's disgust his nephew Alfred became a Roman Catholic, by chance the same nephew was there when Sir Walter was showing Scott some of the curiosities of his museum collection. Sir Walter drew out from the cedar wood cabinet a drawer containing human bones picked up in the Catacombs, and 'The convert lifted them, drawer and all to his nose, and called out, "Oh, they have the odour of sanctity! They are the bones of martyrs!" The face of Sir Walter, expressing impassivity struggling with suppressed derision, was a study, but at last he said, without any perceptible change of voice, "The odour is that of the cedar wood drawer my boy."' Finally he died, as every good hypochondriac should, after an illness of one day in his eighty-third year in the middle of dealing with the morning's post having claimed to the mystification of his doctor on the previous day that tumours were forming on his lungs.

The years spent at Wallington and at the School were on the whole happy years for Scott even if not for Christina; but in the summer of 1858 Mrs Scott invited Christina to stay at their Newcastle home at 4, St Thomas' Crescent for several weeks.[9] Lona Mosk Packer writes[10] 'the Newcastle visit was one of the rare spots of happiness in Christina's life'. Scott invited to meet her at his home Dora Greenwell, the poet, Robert Bewick and Thomas Dixon, amongst others; but the end of the visit and the return to her life in London and the separation from Scott, after being closer to him than ever before, produced the bitter poem, 'Parting After Parting', and the note in Christina's writing in the notebook in which it was written reads, 'In the train from Newcastle, 15th June, 1858'.[11] In 1859 Scott met Alice Boyd and Christina knew final defeat.

In 1863 a reorganization of the School of Design gave Scott the opportunity of resigning his Mastership with a small pension and leaving Newcastle for London. He took the opportunity knowing that for the next three years at least he would be employed by the Department of Science and Art, of the Board

---

[9] I am indebted to Mr Wallace, Newcastle City Librarian and his staff for the information that Scott lived at 4, Wesley Terrace from 1847-1850, at 3, St Thomas' Street from 1850-1857, at 4, St Thomas' Crescent from 1857-1859, and at 14, St Thomas' Crescent from 1859-1864.
[10] *Christina Rossetti* by Lona Mosk Packer at page 121.
[11] op. cit., pp. 121-122.

of Trade, in mural painting and decoration at the South Kensington Museum. As soon as it was known that Scott was going to leave Newcastle, his artisan students raised a subscription fund of their own which reached £30 (a large sum for people of such modest means), and a general subscription open, to the public, brought in much more within days. There is no reason to doubt the sincerity of the comment in the *Newcastle Chronicle* of Saturday, October 3rd, 1863, when it was first announced that Scott was leaving. 'We admire him as an artist and a teacher and we love him as a man. Modest and unobtrusive, genial and intelligent, he has quietly won his way to wide affection.' On 26th November, 1863, a large meeting at the premises of the Literary and Philosophical Society presided over by James Leathart (who under Scott's guidance had for many years been building up his great collection of Pre-Raphaelite paintings), gathered to say farewell to Scott. He was presented with an address from the students of the School (he had already been presented with an address from his former students), and the presentation fund was devoted, on Lady Pauline's suggestion, to commissioning from him a picture (Scott chose as his subject 'The Building of the Old Castle') which was to hang on the stairway of the Literary and Philosophical Society. The Society still has this picture.

On returning to London the final pattern of Scott's life became established. Summer was spent at Penkill Castle, Ayrshire, with Miss Boyd who invited many of Scott's friends as guests including all the Rossettis in turn; by October, like the swallows, they would be preparing to fly south, and Alice Boyd would spend the winter at Scott's London home, Bellevue House, Chelsea, with Mrs Scott. During the winters Scott continued to work for the Department of Science and Art at South Kensington Museum, and acted as Examiner. After 1864 most of his fourteen books on art were written. They showed an immense knowledge and range of interest in the arts—books on Belgian Art, Spanish Art, French Art, Venetian Art, The Little Masters of Germany, a Book on Durer, another on Blake, one on British Sculpture and another on 'British Landscape Painters from Samuel Scott to David Cox'. The books are exceptionally good of their kind, but as Scott wrote, they 'were better than they deserved to be, and only made me feel that I was throwing my time away and was in danger of looking like a literary hack; so I did no more'.

A source of stronger satisfaction to Scott was the publication in 1875 of his 'Ballads, Studies from Nature, Sonnets' with etchings for the book done by Scott and Alma Tadema, the Preface to which discloses only too clearly Scott's uneasy feeling that his credentials to be considered a poet of consequence had not yet, even at that late stage, been established. The volume was received with acclamation by the Rossettis, and by Swinburne, and all Scott's friends, and was then largely forgotten.

Although Scott was by now happy with Alice Boyd, his affection and sympathy for Christina lasted throughout his life. Yet even he must have realized that by casting doubt on Gabriel's mental balance after 1872, 'even such as it had been for many years before', he would cause the devoted sister distress. This is just another paradox of this puzzling Autobiography. His lifelong sympathy is shown by an incident which Lona Packer records.[12] She tells of how on Scott reading Christina's terrible poem 'Summer is Ended'—'a bitter and anguished protest against the inevitable process of ageing which ruthlessly sweeps away a woman's beauty'

> To think that this meaningless thing was ever a rose,
>   Scentless, colourless, *THIS*!

Scott, on reading this expression of despair and self-disgust, sent a poem to Christina with dried rose leaves which was eventually published in the following form:

> Once a rose ever a rose, we say,
>   One we loved and who loved us
> Remains beloved though gone from day;
> To human hearts it must be thus,
>   The past is sweetly laid away.
>
> Sere and sealed for a day and a year,
>   Smell them, dear Christina, pray;

---

[12] See Lona Mosk Packer's *Christina Rossetti*, p. 342 (Cambridge University Press and University of California Press, 1963).

> So nature treats its children dear,
> So memory deals with yesterday,
> The past is sweetly laid away.

However little joy the remaining years held for Christina, life had one more surprise in store for Bell Scott. He describes how in 1881 at the age of seventy, 'without premeditation and with a quite novel feeling of spontaneity, a hundred or more little poems ... came to me fully dressed as it were, every morning between waking and rising. Every day I thought, now the good fairy has exhausted himself, I shall have no more! But still it went on until I had a good many over a hundred, some mornings bringing me two or three.' These poems written in old age and published in 1885 (*A Poet's Harvest Home*), have a moving directness and strength that will keep them young, and a simplicity reminiscent of another if more troubled agnostic—Arthur Hugh Clough. A selection from these poems and other poetry, with some of his prose, would make an Anthology that could win for Scott a new reputation, and lead to a new curiosity about his painting.[13]

A series of heart attacks kept him at Penkill continuously for the last five years of his life, nursed devotedly by Alice Boyd. Mrs Scott came up occasionally to help look after him but for most of the time, with the exception of visits from old friends, Alice Boyd and Scott were alone. His chief occupation was writing letters to his friends, revising his Autobiography and remonstrating with William Rossetti over what he considered William's whitewashing of Gabriel's life. He had a fear of decline, decay and death—the best poem in his 1854 volume written as a young man is called 'Death'—and the theme never failed to inspire real feeling in his poetry. He never wavered in his agnosticism, as had Rossetti to earn Scott's incredulous contempt, and he died on 22nd November, 1890, in his eightieth year in the same stoic and resigned spirit as he had written the poem for his seventieth birthday—

---

[13] Perhaps the curiosity is already here. Quite a small painting, 'The Gloaming, Manse Garden, Berwickshire', brought £1,000 at auction in Newcastle early in 1971.

So many years I've gone this way,
It seems I may walk on for aye,
'Long life God's gift', a brother prayed,
Close on the confines of the dead,
Going reluctant, not afraid:
With bated breath I bow the head
Thinking of those words today.

The ancient tempter well divined
The longing of the sunlit blind,
'Ye shall be wise as gods', he said:
Ah, never may this be, but still
In hope we climb the topless hill.
It is the ending of the strife
Calms and crowns the weary head,
Not till the morn beyond our life
Can the oracle be read,
When the unanswered brain and heart
Hath ceased to ask and ceased to smart:
And all the centuries to come
Like centuries past shall still be dumb.

CHAPTER EIGHT

Jack Common

'I at once came under the minus sign which
society had already placed upon my parents.'
                                    KIDDAR'S LUCK

OF the nine artists whose work is described in this book, only two (William Bell Scott and Thomas Bewick), were born into families with enough money to provide at the outset anything very much more than subsistence and survival. The rest, born into families of working folk and artisans (Avison's mother, a church organist, might consider herself socially superior but her family would be little, if any, better off) had little to protect them from real hardship which, if not immediately present, would be an ever present threat. It is striking, this richness of achievement coming from these Northumbrian homes when contrasted with the relative artistic sterility of the Northumbrian middle class and gentry. It is much the same today, if one remembers the background of Sid Chaplin, Norman Cornish and James Alder.

Perhaps it is because the talent and energy of the more comfortable and assured has gone into the ordering of society. And it must also be true that in the eighteenth and early nineteenth centuries the creative spirit was often devoted to the making of landscape and country house, to gardening, tree planting, and estate management. Yet it is also sad but true that the more assured your own position, the less you may feel the need to prove anything about your society or yourself so that the creative spirit becomes dulled by personal fulfilment. Ironically, it seems that the striving to escape from a narrow and restrictive world is more likely to give rise to artistic achievement than the living of a full life. The rarity of names like Edward Swinburne (the watercolourist) and Algernon Charles Swinburne (the poet), both from Trollap's Capheaton, Pauline, Lady Trevelyan from Wallington, and Joseph Crawhall, only strengthens the argument.

But there is a terrible price that the artist frequently pays for his release from restriction through creative success. Taste, imagination, sensibility and the critical faculty, must often divorce him from his own people; yet he may never feel much or any sympathy with the values and way of life of any other class or group—indeed, he may detest them. This is the limbo world, the no man's land in which some artists live, so that frustration of a different kind is felt after success is won. It is even worse when the achievement is there with the frustration, but the recognition and success is denied. That is what happened to Jack Common.

He was born, the son of a Newcastle railwayman, in 1903 in an upstairs railway flat in Third Avenue, in the suburb of Heaton, and was to become, in addition to several other things, a solicitor's office boy, a mechanic, a shop assistant, an intimate friend of George Orwell and the author of two neglected autobiographical novels which should have won him a wide acclaim—and did not.

After leaving his Heaton school at the age of fourteen, the boy—who had shone at nothing except his English essays which the Headmaster read out to the whole school—went to a Commercial College and took a job in a solicitor's office at 12/6 a week; but in the early twenties the Royal Arcade, where many political groups—differing only in their degree of unreality used to meet, and where the People's Theatre group was founded—provided the only free education after the age of fourteen then available in Newcastle; and it was there that the young Common cut his intellectual teeth before leaving Newcastle for London in the late twenties to stake his claim to a place in the literary world.

In 1932 he became the Assistant Editor of John Middleton Murry's *Adelphi* and in 1935 for a short time was appointed Editor. After that he worked for film units as a script writer and Literary Adviser and turned his hand to a variety of sad things.

In 1938 he edited and wrote the introduction to 'Seven Shifts', a study of men at work in a particular kind of society. In the same year the same publishers, Secker and Warburg, published his essays on the political and cultural convulsions of his time called 'The Freedom of the Streets'. In his review of this book in the *New English Weekly*,[1] George Orwell wrote, 'This is the authentic voice of the ordinary man, the man who might infuse a new decency into the control of affairs if only he could get there, but who in practice never seems to get much further than the trenches, the sweatshop and the jail'. In 1951 *Kiddar's Luck* was published and in 1954 *The Ampersand*—its companion volume and sequel. In 1968 he died.

Kiddar's Luck is the story of Jack Common's first fourteen years of growing up in the Newcastle of the early 1900s up to 1917. Nearly all the background facts in Kiddar are true, his mother's limp, his father's giant stature, and the detailed description of the very house and street in which he lived. He sees through a child's eyes, the teeming activity in street and back lane, the scramble of vans, barrows, milk chariots, coal carts, steam wagons, the milkman's handbell, the Cullercoats fishwives' cry, the rag and bone man's bugle, the firewood seller's wail and the whole hierarchy of old people, adults, relatives, boys' and girls' street games and the place of the newly born—a whole culture that has gone;

> 'Everybody's washing hung across the lane, so that the appearance of a tradesman's cart meant a rush to tuck sheets and things round the rope and to raise the diminished bunting high over the horse's head with a prop. The coal-man was the biggest menace, since a mere brush against his tarry sacks meant a second washing-day. At his cry every housewife instantly rushed out to struggle with the props, and down the lane you'd see one line of sheets after another shoot up a couple of yards and the horse's head appear very black beneath the sky-flung whiteness. Naturally bad lads learnt to imitate his cry. They'd conceal themselves behind the last line of washing, and give vent to a convincing "Coal ter wagon!", then wait for the scamper.'

'Kiddar' tells of the boy's growing up in these streets, his

[1] 16th June, 1938.

growing humiliation at his mother's drinking, and his realization that his parents' marriage is falling apart.

Of Kiddar, Sid Chaplin wrote—[2]

> 'There are four chapters alone on life before age five, a miracle of total recall including a description of how it feels to be a bairn in a pram with the sun kissing your face, or crawling and registering every detail of the furniture, every sound and smell in an Edwardian kitchen or seeing Mrs Buchan swilling beer from a jug or granny dead in her coffin ...
>
> ... He is indeed the nearest anybody ever got to Charlie Chaplin in print ... the sentences skid and dance and hop on one leg or take a custard pie right on the chin or duck and weave and leave you gasping behind. But he is more for the wry smile than the belly laugh.'

Hard times came to Jack Common after 1945 and in a letter to Irene Palmer dated 10th December, 1950, he tells of the circumstances under which Kiddar is being written:

> 'I am as thin as a rake, yes I am you know: terribly sober; a six in the morning riser; and a worker all the hours there are. These read like the qualifications for a very poor job. And I had three till a month ago. From seven till five, I was a labourer plying a nimble shovel (well sometimes nimble); seven till ten, a critic compiling film reports; Sat and Sun afternoons an author writing his books ... I thought of tendering my resignation. But you know I have never resigned from anything all my life. However, I got the sack—that is more in keeping with my tradition. So now I turn out three film reports on books every week which takes me till Thursday and earns me £4 10s. and then I turn to the book. It should be finished as per contract, by the end of the year—publishers, if and when, Turnstile Press.'

And later (2nd April, 1951) to the same correspondent ...

> 'I finished my book only two weeks behind schedule despite

---

[2] 'A Farewell to Jack Common', *Sunday Times* 1968.

my five months hard labour at the nursery and the production of some 50,000 words of film reporting. Simultaneously with people snatching the roof off my head and turning out the electric light and littering me with summonses, and my typewriter breaking down in all directions and lack of beer thinning my blood, lack of tobacco making my lungs transparent—Irene, never was book writ before in such a ringing set of circumstances.'

Of these circumstances there is no trace in Kiddar. The writing is without a trace of self-pity and the witty and ironic style is best appreciated by being read aloud: here is his description of the blunder he made as an unborn babe in the choosing of his parents.

'... it's the operation I was about to take part in one cold November night in the year 1902 when me and my genes were barging about on the other side of time, corporally uncommitted and the whole world of chance open to us. It was then that we made a mess of things.

There were plenty of golden opportunities going that night. In palace and mansion flat, in hall and manor and new central-heated "cottage", the wealthy, talented and beautiful lay coupled—welcome wombs were ten-a-penny, must have been. What do you think I picked on, me and my genes, that is? Missing lush Sussex, the Surrey soft spots, affluent Mayfair and gold-filled Golder's Green, ... I came upon the frost-rimmed roofs of a working-class suburb in Newcastle-upon-Tyne, and in the back bedroom of an upstairs flat in a street parallel with the railway line, on which a halted engine whistled to be let through the junction, I chose my future parents. There, it was done. By the time that engine took its rightaway and rolled into the blue glare of the junction arcs, another kiddar was started, an event, one might add, of no novelty in that quarter and momentous only to me.

I at once came under the minus-sign which society had already placed upon my parents. They were of no account, not even overdrawn or marked "R.D.", people who worked for a living and got just that, who had a home only so long as they paid the weekly rent, and who could provide for offspring by the simple method of doing without themselves. I had picked the bottom rung of the ladder with a vengeance, for it was that kind of ladder used in the imaginations of mathematicians, on which the rungs mount in minus degrees and the top is crowned with no opulence of over-plus but with the mere integer. A sad mistake; though millions make it I think it still deserves a mourning wreath.'

Most of the writing is of the same quality, right through to the final pages of savage self-mockery bringing both childhood and book to an end in 1917 when he writes an imaginary letter to his future employer:

'Dear Sir,
With reference to your advertisement ... I beg to apply for the post. I am fourteen years of age, strong, healthy, bright, punctual, clean and willing. My parents are working class, my environment is working class, the school I have just left is working class, and with your kind assistance I feel qualified to become working class myself.

Because I have known poverty, I am certain to accept the small wage you intend to offer. Because I resent poverty, I am likely to join any organization or activity which has the object of making you pay bigger wages. Because I know how poverty cripples the humble, I intend to be ambitious, within limits, and ready to advance myself at your expense ... as a member from birth of the community of the streets I am aware that individual success for one of our sort, if contrived and not accidental, incurs a personal severance from the rest. That makes a man ridiculous, you know. The self-promoted working man is as much a living anomaly as the wealthy priest, the socially approved poet, the knighted scientist, or the bearded lady. Hedged off, therefore as I am from a conventional or an infamous success by these parallel electric fences, it is probable I shall tread the daily round for a regular pittance all my life—that suits you ...'

And in between describing the blunder of his birth and this bitter leave-taking of childhood, there is an unforgettable gallery of 'ordinary' people, drawn sharp as a needle—whole streets of them, eccentrics and relatives, drawn with such truth you feel you have met them—and if you live on Tyneside and are over fifty, you probably have.

Here is one of them:

'My Aunt Mary Jane ... she was a tidier-upper, she was. Her whole life was a fearful struggle against the Apollyon of Dirt, or "Dort" as she pronounced it. Anybody but herself would have said she was the victor. Not her. She would see "dort" on surfaces that to the uninstructed eye had been polished down to a new skin of cleanliness. "Dort" was always creeping in behind her, following after her broom and breeding even where the duster had just left off ... The working class wife who really goes in for cleanliness, as plenty do, especially if she has no children, keeps a home which easily outshines any in the country. People of the other classes have largely lost their standards in this matter ... The true graft of scrupulous dirt-hatred is not there. In the middle class home one is nearly always aware of a latent dinginess ... it is a safe bet that the corners, the places in shadows have been skipped; the swift wipe of polish doesn't really cover up the lack of scrubbing ... gardening she left to her husband. But the house—"hoose" she called it—was her supreme concern. When I was allowed inside it I had the sensation of coming into a glass palace. Breathe and you left a stain. Uncle Bill always arrived by the back-door, where he took off his boots and stepped in his socks from one bit of newspaper to another until he arrived at his seat left side of the hearth. There he sat most evenings, his feet still on newspaper ...

Aunt Mary Jane studied the deaths. Any of the Northumbrian names, Charlton or Foster or Twizell say, set her speculating on who the deceased could be. She and her husband were related to half the clans on the border; she couldn't realize that names once localized had gone into the city melting pot and were becoming meaningless as indications of the owner's clan-membership. For example, when my father complained once that a watch-maker called Forster had made an unsatisfactory job of mending his watch—"Ay," says she, "the Forsters were always a bad lot. Ye should ha known better than take it theor" ... So they sat most evenings in the showcase of a room surrounded by reflecting surfaces and under the presidency of a proud and glittering grandfather clock which always seemed to me to be saying "NO DORT, NO DORT".'

Jack Common preferred Kiddar's sequel, *The Ampersand*, which carries his story on after the age of fourteen and which book again is neglected and out of print. In a letter he said 'I'm trying to get them (Turnstile Press) to give me an advance on my next, which IS a masterpiece'. Yet some devilish impulse of self-denigration (which was typical) made him change the surname of the boy from KIDDAR to CLARTS—although the father remained the same railwayman father and the mother the same limping mother. Kiddar, as we all should know, is the affectionate Geordie word for Boy—any older brother will refer to any younger brother as 'Our Kiddar'—whilst Clarts is a Geordie word with derisive overtones for Mud or Muck or a mixture of both.

This book has the same rare writing as 'Kiddar'. Here is the description of the Solicitor's office on his first Monday morning there—

'Then the air of the office met them. It had died in there over the weekend. The atmosphere was yellowish with yesterday's slain sunbeams, still tepid with the warmth of their decomposing, and its burden of a fine dust, too thick to be merely a scent, too rich to be less than a taste, testified to the further demise of old deeds and dry volumes ...

... this was the epitome and concentrate of documentary catacombs. The atmosphere in this place had never been alive, surely. It must have come from mummys' lungs originally, and then hung in millennial stillness about dry Egyptian tombs. It stayed inert about a single electric light bulb ... it was the aspic in which sundry black deedboxes with names like tombstones found eternity ... He wanted to get out at once. Why, you could die in here easily and you'd never rot, not perceptibly or in a century or two.'

Both books are heavily flavoured with sentences and ideas that stay in the mind—

'Boredom or the ability to endure it, is the hub on which the whole universe of work turns. The genius and the chimpanzee are impatient of it, and here and there in a civilized society occur individuals who hark back to these ancestral types and are resistant to scholarship ... Most of us, however, are unable to survive being educated. We learn reading and boredom, writing and boredom, arithmetic and boredom, and so on ... till in the end it is quite certain you can put us to the most boring job there is and we'll endure it.'

'When she explained that thunder was God's anger against the wicked ... my father pooh-poohed all this ... why did they have lightning conductors on churches? Couldn't they trust the Almighty's aim? Grandma would murmur darkly about the wicked in their pride, and though he stood there large and confident as ever I thought myself he was taking a risk.'

'Anyone who has ever had close dealings with women must have been struck by the curious knack they have of being impossibly in the right, and genuinely so, just at that point when you think you really have got them. They get murdered for this, frequently, but it still is so.'

'Newcastle being a fine town to roam in ... since it is all hills, vales, bridges, and one view succeeds another every hundred paces in a manner which fascinates anyone with an eye for composition in a landscape. True, for two centuries or more the main endeavour of the city fathers has been to destroy this balance ... Still, there is a natural obduracy in the configuration of the place which resists all the erosions and excrescences which otherwise must have made a Hull or Birmingham of it.'

I have said that these books are neglected—but there has always been a minority of writers and others who have appreciated them and lent out their rare copies. And Common's literary friends encouraged him by making clear to him how much they admired his writing. He repaid them by talk, hours of talk, on beer (on which he could show astonishing erudition), on politics, on art, on anything in the world that roused his anger or enthusiasm or appealed to his sense of the ridiculous. But his talk, although precious, took up much time that should have been spent in writing. It will be noticed that in a life of sixty-five years the two books for which he will be remembered (if some publisher can be persuaded to get them made accessible to the public again) were written between 1949 and 1954—a period of five years. He believed in himself—but only intermittently; and his self-destructive and self-deprecating sense of humour although very funny masked a nightmare sense of despair and disgust. In a letter referring to the death of a child he wrote "—a senseless calamity which brings one up against the awful grin behind the universe ... Everyone has their own technique for producing the boozy half-blindness which is the first condition for continued living. They'll have a way likely, a better way than I have. In any case, there's no talking to the lightning-struck, the fatally-illuminated are always alone.'

Wishing for literary recognition, knowing he deserved it, feeling contempt for the self-promoting salesmanship by which it is so often achieved, he never would in any event take himself for long with that sufficient degree of seriousness which is so helpful. Self-derision would keep breaking in. And even had he won success, the painful honesty that went into the making of Will Kiddar and Clarts would not have allowed him to be satisfied and fooled by it—any more than was Siegfried Sassoon—

> 'I saw that smiling conjurer Success—
> An impresario in full evening dress—
> Advancing towards me from some floodlit place
> Where Fame resides. I did not like his face.
>
> I did not like this too forthcoming chap
> Whose programme was "to put me on the map"
> Therefore I left his blandishments unheeded,
> And told him I was not the man he needed.'

In *The Ampersand*, there is a description of the boy's realization that he is different to others, and why, and he feels a terrible sense of loss as well as gain:

'The sight of those good folk going home somehow inverted his mood. He had now an immense awareness of the living community around him and felt the apartness that gave it him to be an amputation. And so it was indeed. His similars among the more fortunate classes are not likely to be put to so extreme a severance when their nature shows itself. They can usually be drafted into an intelligentsia that is well organized, tolerated, even socially blessed. This is only an oasis they are in perhaps; it isn't wilderness. But Bill Clarts, coming this cold night from the small room of a lonely, thinking man, contraband books under his arm, felt himself engaged in a traffic which must alienate him from his kind.

Suddenly he didn't want that ... the presence of the sleepy hosts around felt like a claim upon him. He was drawn to this huge, mute community that lay shut up in half-houses, family by family, under the uniform tile, each of them maintaining a warm hearth against all hazards by the slender defence of a weekly wage.

... Clarts merely fumbled with these premonitions. What he knew was that he wanted both to be good with his kind and at the same time fulfil the separate needs of his nature. Uncle Rod's solution of the problem was to be a crank. But a working class crank was really a kind of city-idiot.'

No writer's growing awareness of the conflict between his background and his art has ever, it seems to me, been better expressed. The tragedy is, that even as he takes up his pen to write the great novel, the divide between himself and his own people will widen. Yet in these two books, at a cost to himself which only he could know, passing judgement from a lonely distance on himself and his parents with a passionate impartiality, Jack Common catches the very sound and sight and smell of growing up on Tyneside fifty years ago.

It would be good to believe (if there is any literary justice in the world), that so far as the books are concerned, that minus sign will turn out to be a plus sign after all. I believe that it will, and that these books will be enjoyed as long as there are people on the banks of the Tyne who retain an interest in their past and value what makes their region unique. I have tried to avoid describing these books as masterpieces but in the end I have to say that is precisely what they are.